Emeril Lagasse Power Air Fryer 360 Cookbook for Beginners

300 Quick and Easy Everyday Recipes for Healthier Fried Favorites （30-Day Meal Plan）

Jennifie Rossen

Table of Contents

Introduction

Air fryer ovens have been a popular kitchen gadget in the last few years because of their compact size, versatility, and capability to cook a different range of recipes into a single cooking appliance. The Emeril Lagasse Power Air Fryer 360 is one of the advanced and multipurpose cooking appliances available in the market. It is 9 in 1 cooking appliance that comes with 12-different preset functions like air fry, roast, rotisserie, bagel, pizza, slow cook, broil, warm, dehydrate, reheat, bake and toast. You can choose preset from these functions as per your recipe needs.

The Emeril Lagasse power air fryer 360 equipped with advanced 360° airflow technology to cook your food faster and gives you even and crispy cooking results all time. The Emeril Lagasse power air fryer takes you to stress out from cooking so you can enjoy your food with your friends and family members. The Emeril Lagasse power not only saves your time and money but also makes your daily cooking process easier and convenient way.

This cookbook contains different types of recipes like breakfast, poultry, beef, pork & lamb, fish & seafood, vegetables & side dishes, snacks & appetizers, dehydrate, and desserts. The recipes written in this cookbook are unique and written in an easily understandable form. All the recipes are written with their preparation and cooking time with step by step cooking instructions. Each and every recipe is written in this book is ends with their nutritional value information. The nutritional value information will help you to keep track of daily calorie intake. The book also comes with a 30-days meal plan. Planning your meal helps you to keep track of how much you have to eat. There are few books available in the market on these topics thanks for choosing my book. I hope you love and enjoy all the recipes written in this book.

Chapter 1: Basics of Emeril Lagasse Power Air Fryer 360

Emeril Lagasse Power Air Fryer 360 is one of the first products developed by Sequential Brand Group, Inc and Tristar Products, Inc with the partnership. They have introduced a power air fryer 360 multipurpose cooking appliances made-up from stainless steel body. It works on 1500 watt and comes with five heating elements which cook your food faster and gives your even cooking results.

The Emeril Lagasse Power Air Fryer 360 is a versatile cooking appliance loaded with 12 preset cooking functions like Air fry, rotisserie, toast, roast, bagel, slow cook, bake, dehydrate, reheat, broil, pizza, and warm. You can use these functions as per your cooking needs. Its 360 air crisp technology circulates super-heated airflow creates a whirlwind to make your food crisper from outside and tender from inside. Due to its large size capacity, it is capable to hold the whole turkey for roasting, dehydrate fruits and vegetable slices, toast 6 slices of bread, air fry chicken, bake pizza, and more. The oven comes with different accessories like a baking pan, frying basket, drip tray, crisper tray, pizza rack, and rotisserie split.

The oven comes with 4 different cooking slot positions you can choose these slots as per your recipe needs like the first position slot position is ideal for dehydrating and broiling your food. The second position slot is used to air fry, roast, broil, dehydrate, rotisserie, and bagel functions. The third position slot is used to bake, roast, warm, pizza, reheat, and dehydrate functions. The last fourth position is ideal for slow cooking purposes. The memory feature of the oven allows recalling the last used time and temperature settings set by the user. To cook multiple food items the oven is capable to hold two layers of pan or basket at once. The large front glass windows allow you to monitor your food during the cooking process.

Common Functions of Emeril Lagasse Power Air Fryer 360

The Emeril Lagasse power air fryer is loaded with a big LCD display which helps to choose the time, temperature, and functions with dial and touch buttons. When the oven is in selection or standby mode the display illuminates Blue light and when the cooking process is in progress it illuminates Orange light. All these controls and their functions are given below.

- TEMP/DARKNESS Dial

This dialler is used to change the preset temperature settings as per recipe needs. It is also used to set the darkness level while using the bagel or toast function. Using this dial you can easily adjust the temperature settings during the current cooking process.

- TIME/SLICES Dial

Using this dial you can easily change preset time settings as per recipe needs. It is also used to set the number of slices while using the bagel or toast function. The dial allows you to change time settings during the current cooking process.

- SELECT Dial

Using this dial you can easily select the desire preset cooking functions shows on display.

- AIR FRY Button

While using Air fry, bake, slow cook, reheat, pizza rotisserie, roast, and dehydrate functions you can use this button to activate the internal fan. The fan blows very hot air into the cooking chamber using 360 airflow technology to gives you crispy and tender cooking results. Using this function you can cook your favorite fried food like snacks and main dishes with very little oil.

- LIGHT Button

You can press this button any time during the cooking process to see or monitor your food.

- °F/°C Button

Using this button you can easily select your proffered temperature measuring method.

- START/PAUSE Button

Using this button you can start the new cooking program or you can pause the current working program.

- CANCEL Button

Using this button you can stop the current cooking process at any time. You can also use this button to power off the main unit by continuously pressing the CANCEL button for 3 seconds.

Preset Functions of Emeril Lagasse Power Air Fryer 360

The Emeril Lagasse power air fryer comes with 12-preset cooking functions. While using these functions you never need to worry about the time and temperature settings all preset or you can recall your last used settings using these functions.

1. Air Fry: This is one of the healthy cooking functions used to air fry your favorite foods like snacks with very little oil. Using this function you can make your food crispy from the outside and tender, juicy from the inside.

   - First set the crispier tray at the 4th rack position.
   - The heat comes from side heating elements.
   - While using this function air fryer fan is always on.

2. Toast: Using this function you can easily toast your white or brown bread. It makes your bread brown and nice crisp on both sides.

   - First set the pizza rack at the 2nd rack position.
   - Select the desire darkness level between 1-5.
   - Select the desired number of bread slices between 1-6.

3. Bagel: This function works the same as the toast function. You need to set your bagel slice over the pizza rack. It makes your bagel nice crisp and brown on both sides.

   - First set the pizza rack at the 2nd rack position.
   - Select the desire darkness level between 1-5.
   - Select the desired number of bagel slices between 1-6.

4. Pizza: Using this function you can make a perfect homemade pizza or you can also make frozen pizza.

   - First set the pizza rack at the 5th rack position.
   - While using this function air fryer fan is always on.

5. Bake: This function is ideal for baking your favorite cake, cookies, pastries, pies, and more.

   - First set your baking tray or pizza rack at the 5th rack position.
   - While using this function air fryer fan can turn off.

6. **Broil:** Using this function you can broil your favorite sandwiches or melt cheese over burgers.

   - First set your baking pan or pizza rack on 1st or 2nd rack position.
   - While using this function air fryer fan can turn off.

7. **Rotisserie:** It is also known as the split roasting method to roast your whole chicken using rotisserie tools. It makes your chicken crisp from the outside and tender, juicy from the inside.

   - Use rotisserie split accessories and set it at the 3rd rotisserie slot position.
   - While using this function air fryer fan can turn off.

8. **Slow Cook:** This function cooks your food for a longer time especially great for tough meat cuts. It makes your tough meats tender and juicy.

   - First set the pizza rack at 6th position.
   - While using this function air fryer fan is always on.

9. **Roast:** This function is ideal for roasting a large piece of poultry or meat and it gives even cooking results.

   - First set pizza rack at 5th rack position.
   - While using this function air fryer fan is always on.

10. **Dehydrate:** Using this function you can dehydrate your favorite meat, vegetable, and fruit slices.

    - First set the crisper tray at 1st, 4th, and 5th position.
    - While using this function air fryer fan is always on.

11. **Reheat:** Using this function you can reheat your food without searing.

    - First set pizza rack at 5th rack position.
    - While using this function air fryer fan is always on.

12. **Warm:** This setting is ideal to keep your food warm by maintaining a safe temperature (160°F) until it is ready to serve.

    - First set baking pan, pizza rack, or crisper tray at 5th rack position.
    - While using this function air fryer fan can turn off.

Benefits of Air Fryer Oven

The air fryer oven comes with various benefits some of the important benefits are given as follows:

1. Versatile cooking appliance

The air fryer oven comes with various different kinds of functions in a single appliance. You can use it as an air fryer, toaster, oven, and more no need to purchase a separate appliance for single cooking functions.

2. Use less oil

Air fryer oven requires very less oil for daily cooking less oil. There are numerous advantages to using less oil, the first advantage is it is an economical way to cook your favorite food. Less oil means fewer calories so it is one of the healthier cooking methods. Less oil means less mess so it is easy to clean.

3. Healthier than deep-frying

The air frying method is one of the healthier methods compare with the traditional deep frying method. The food cooked using the air frying method is low in fats and calories. It is also lower in the harmful compounds founds in traditional deep frying food. If you want to lose weight without cutting the fried food then switching to an air fryer is one of the best choices for you.

4. Large cooking capacity

The air fryer oven is a multipurpose cooking appliance that comes with a large cooking capacity. It is capable to hold 10 lb of chicken for roasting, 6 slices of bread for toasting, bake a pizza, air frying chicken and you can use the two trays at a different position to cook a large quantity of food.

5. Easy to clean

Air fryer cooks your food with less oil so less oil means less mess. The air fryer comes with removable accessories and most of them are dishwasher safe. You just need to remove the drip tray by sliding it out then wash or rinse it with water and wipe off with a clean and dry cloth.

Cleaning and Maintenance

To clean and maintain your Emeril Lagasse Power Air Fryer 360 you need to follow the simple cleaning steps given below.

1. Before starting the actual cleaning method first unplug your air fryer oven from the power socket and let it cool down at room temperature.
2. Then remove the accessories like a crisper tray, pizza rack, drip tray, rotisserie split, and baking pan, etc. All these accessories are dishwasher safe you can wash them in the dishwasher or use soapy water to clean the accessories.
3. Then clean the main unit from outside with the help of mild detergent and moist cloth. Clean the oven door with the help of soapy water and a damp cloth. Do not immerse the power air fryer main unit in water. It is not dishwasher safe because electric parts and heating elements are present in the main unit.
4. Clean the interior of the oven with the help of hot water, a non-abrasive sponge, and a damp clean cloth. Do not scrub the heating elements if necessary use a non-abrasive cleaning brush to clean any food residue.
5. Make sure all the accessories are thoroughly dry before assembling them with the main unit. Now your oven is ready for next use.

Chapter 2: Breakfast

Greek Egg Muffins

Preparation Time: 10 minutes
Cooking Time: 20 minutes
Serve: 6
Ingredients:

- 6 eggs
- 1/3 cup feta cheese, crumbled
- 1/4 cup fresh basil, chopped
- 1/3 cup sun-dried tomatoes, chopped
- Pepper
- Salt

Directions:

1. Spray muffin pan with cooking spray and set aside.
2. In a bowl, whisk eggs with tomatoes, feta cheese, basil, pepper, and salt.
3. Pour egg mixture into the muffin pan.
4. Select bake mode. Set the temperature to 375 F and the timer for 20 minutes. Press start.
5. Let the air fryer preheat then insert the pizza rack into shelf position 5.
6. Place muffin pan on the pizza rack and cook.
7. Serve and enjoy.

Nutritional Value (Amount per Serving):

- Calories 87
- Fat 6.2 g
- Carbohydrates 1.1 g
- Sugar 0.9 g
- Protein 6.8 g
- Cholesterol 171 mg

Spinach Pepper Egg Muffins

Preparation Time: 10 minutes
Cooking Time: 25 minutes
Serve: 12
Ingredients:

- 2 cups egg whites
- 12 olives, pitted & chopped
- 2 roasted red peppers, chopped
- 2 cups baby spinach, chopped
- 2 green onions, chopped
- 1/4 cup feta cheese, crumbled
- Pepper
- Salt

Directions:

1. Spray 12-cups muffin pan with cooking spray and set aside.
2. Divide evenly olives, pepper, and spinach in a muffin pan cup.
3. In a bowl, whisk egg whites with green onions, crumbled cheese, pepper, and salt.
4. Pour egg mixture into the prepared muffin pan.
5. Select bake mode. Set the temperature to 350 F and the timer for 25 minutes. Press start.
6. Let the air fryer preheat then insert the pizza rack into shelf position 5.
7. Place muffin pan on the pizza rack and cook.
8. Serve and enjoy.

Nutritional Value (Amount per Serving):

- Calories 40
- Fat 1.3 g
- Carbohydrates 1.8 g
- Sugar 1 g
- Protein 5.2 g
- Cholesterol 3 mg

Healthy Spinach Frittata

Preparation Time: 10 minutes
Cooking Time: 20 minutes
Serve: 6

Ingredients:

- 6 eggs
- 1/2 cup frozen spinach, defrosted & drained
- 1/4 cup feta cheese, crumbled
- 1/2 cup olives, chopped
- 1/2 cup tomatoes, diced
- 1/2 tsp garlic powder
- 1 tsp oregano
- 1/4 cup milk
- 1/4 tsp salt

Directions:

1. Spray a 9-inch baking pan with cooking spray and set aside.
2. In a bowl, whisk eggs with oregano, garlic powder, milk, pepper, and salt until well combined.
3. Add olives, feta, tomatoes, and spinach and stir well.
4. Pour egg mixture into the prepared baking pan.
5. Select bake mode. Set the temperature to 400 F and the timer for 20 minutes. Press start.
6. Let the air fryer preheat then insert the pizza rack into shelf position 5.
7. Place baking pan on the pizza rack and cook.
8. Serve and enjoy.

Nutritional Value (Amount per Serving):

- Calories 102
- Fat 7.2 g
- Carbohydrates 2.8 g
- Sugar 1.5 g
- Protein 7.1 g
- Cholesterol 170 mg

Quinoa Veggie Egg Muffins

Preparation Time: 10 minutes
Cooking Time: 25 minutes
Serve: 6
Ingredients:
- 3 eggs
- 1 1/2 cups mixed vegetables, cooked
- 1/2 cup feta cheese, crumbled
- 1 cup egg whites
- 1/2 cup fresh parsley, chopped
- 1 tbsp onion powder
- 1 cup cooked quinoa
- Pepper
- Salt

Directions:
1. Spray muffin pan with cooking spray and set aside.
2. In a large bowl, whisk egg whites and eggs.
3. Add remaining ingredients and stir well.
4. Pour egg mixture into the prepared muffin pan.
5. Select bake mode. Set the temperature to 350 F and the timer for 25 minutes. Press start.
6. Let the air fryer preheat then insert the pizza rack into shelf position 5.
7. Place baking pan on the pizza rack and cook.
8. Serve and enjoy.

Nutritional Value (Amount per Serving):
- Calories 218
- Fat 6.8 g
- Carbohydrates 24.8 g
- Sugar 1.4 g
- Protein 14.1 g
- Cholesterol 93 mg

Tomato Spinach Egg Muffins

Preparation Time: 10 minutes
Cooking Time: 20 minutes
Serve: 6
Ingredients:
- 3 eggs
- 1/4 cup cheddar cheese, grated

- 1 tomato, chopped
- 1/4 cup leek, chopped
- 1/4 cup parmesan cheese, grated
- 2 tbsp milk
- 1/4 bell pepper, chopped
- 1/2 cup baby spinach, chopped
- Pepper
- Salt

Directions:

1. Spray 6-cups muffin pan with cooking spray and set aside.
2. In a bowl, whisk eggs with cheese and milk. Add remaining ingredients and stir well.
3. Pour egg mixture into the prepared muffin pan.
4. Select bake mode. Set the temperature to 350 F and the timer for 20 minutes. Press start.
5. Let the air fryer preheat then insert the pizza rack into shelf position 5.
6. Place muffin pan on the pizza rack and cook.
7. Serve and enjoy.

Nutritional Value (Amount per Serving):

- Calories 71
- Fat 4.7 g
- Carbohydrates 2 g
- Sugar 1.1 g
- Protein 5.6 g
- Cholesterol 90 mg

Healthy Artichoke Frittata

Preparation Time: 10 minutes
Cooking Time: 25 minutes
Serve: 6
Ingredients:

- 10 eggs
- 14 oz marinated artichoke hearts, drained & quartered
- 2 tbsp olive oil
- 1 cup mozzarella cheese, grated
- 1 tbsp Dijon mustard
- 1 tsp garlic, minced
- 5 cups baby spinach
- 1/2 cup sour cream
- 1/4 tsp pepper
- 1 tsp kosher salt

Directions:

1. In a large bowl, whisk eggs with sour cream, 1/2 cup cheese, mustard, pepper, and salt. Set aside.
2. Heat oil in a pan over medium heat.
3. Add artichokes and cook for 8 minutes.

4. Add garlic and spinach and cook until spinach is wilted.
5. Transfer vegetable mixture into the baking dish.
6. Pour egg mixture over vegetables and sprinkle with remaining cheese.
7. Select bake mode. Set the temperature to 400 F and the timer for 25 minutes. Press start.
8. Let the air fryer preheat then insert the pizza rack into shelf position 5.
9. Place baking dish on the pizza rack and cook.
10. Serve and enjoy.

Nutritional Value (Amount per Serving):
- Calories 280
- Fat 23 g
- Carbohydrates 6.1 g
- Sugar 1.4 g
- Protein 12.7 g
- Cholesterol 284 mg

Healthy Breakfast Muffins

Preparation Time: 10 minutes
Cooking Time: 30 minutes
Serve: 12
Ingredients:
- 2 cups oat flour
- 1 tsp vanilla
- 1/3 cup butter, melted
- 1/2 cup maple syrup
- 1 cup applesauce
- 1 tsp cinnamon
- 2 tsp baking powder
- 1/4 tsp salt

Directions:
1. Line muffin pan with muffin liners.
2. In a bowl, add applesauce, cinnamon, vanilla, melted butter, maple syrup, and salt and stir to combine.
3. Add baking powder and oat flour and stir well to mix.
4. Spoon batter into the prepared muffin pan.
5. Select bake mode. Set the temperature to 350 F and the timer for 30 minutes. Press start.
6. Let the air fryer preheat then insert the pizza rack into shelf position 5.
7. Place muffin pan on the pizza rack and cook.
8. Allow cooling completely.
9. Serve and enjoy.

Nutritional Value (Amount per Serving):
- Calories 151
- Fat 6.2 g

- Carbohydrates 22.2 g
- Sugar 9.9 g
- Protein 2.1 g
- Cholesterol 14 mg

Pumpkin Steel Cut Oats

Preparation Time: 10 minutes
Cooking Time: 8 hours
Serve: 6
Ingredients:

- 1 cup steel-cut oats
- 2 cups of milk
- 2 1/2 cups water
- 2 tsp ground cinnamon
- 2 tsp pumpkin pie spice
- 2 tbsp chia seeds
- 1/4 cup maple syrup
- 1 cup pumpkin puree

Directions:

1. Add all ingredients into the dutch oven and cover with a lid.
2. Insert the pizza rack into shelf position 6.
3. Place dutch oven on pizza rack.
4. Select a slow cook mode. Set the temperature to 225 F and the timer for 8 hours. Press start.
5. Stir well and serve.

Nutritional Value (Amount per Serving):

- Calories 166
- Fat 5.4 g
- Carbohydrates 25.8 g
- Sugar 13 g
- Protein 5.7 g
- Cholesterol 7 mg

Healthy Almond Oatmeal

Preparation Time: 10 minutes
Cooking Time: 35 minutes
Serve: 4
Ingredients:

- 2 cups old fashioned oats
- 1/2 cup almond butter
- 1 3/4 cup milk
- 2 tsp vanilla
- 1/4 cup maple syrup
- 1/4 tsp salt

Directions:

1. Spray a baking dish with cooking spray and set aside.

2. In a large bowl, whisk milk, vanilla, maple syrup, almond butter, and salt. Add oats and stir to mix.
3. Pour oats mixture into the prepared baking dish.
4. Select bake mode. Set the temperature to 375 F and the timer for 35 minutes. Press start.
5. Let the air fryer preheat then insert the pizza rack into shelf position 5.
6. Place baking dish on the pizza rack and cook.
7. Serve and enjoy.

Nutritional Value (Amount per Serving):
- Calories 435
- Fat 8.5 g
- Carbohydrates 72.8 g
- Sugar 19 g
- Protein 13.9 g
- Cholesterol 9 mg

Blueberry Oats

Preparation Time: 10 minutes
Cooking Time: 7 hours
Serve: 6
Ingredients:
- 1 cup steel-cut oats
- 1/2 cup quinoa, rinsed
- 1 tbsp butter, melted
- 1 tbsp lemon zest
- 1 tsp vanilla
- 1 cup blueberries
- 2 tbsp maple syrup
- 5 cups of water
- 1/4 tsp salt

Directions:
1. Add all ingredients into the dutch oven and stir everything well.
2. Cover the dutch oven with a lid.
3. Insert the pizza rack into shelf position 6.
4. Place dutch oven on pizza rack.
5. Select a slow cook mode. Set the temperature to 225 F and the timer for 7 hours. Press start.
6. Stir well and serve.

Nutritional Value (Amount per Serving):
- Calories 131
- Fat 3.5 g
- Carbohydrates 22 g
- Sugar 6.6 g
- Protein 3.2 g
- Cholesterol 5 mg

Sweet Potato Muffins

Preparation Time: 10 minutes
Cooking Time: 25 minutes
Serve: 12
Ingredients:

- 2 1/2 cups sweet potatoes, cooked and mashed
- 1/2 cup coconut sugar
- 1 1/2 cups whole wheat flour
- 1/2 tsp vanilla
- 1 tsp ground cinnamon
- 3 tsp baking powder
- 3/4 cup milk
- Pinch of salt

Directions:

1. Line muffin pan with muffin liners and set aside.
2. Add mashed sweet potatoes, vanilla, and milk to the blender and blend until smooth.
3. In a large bowl, mix flour, cinnamon, baking powder, coconut sugar, and salt.
4. Add sweet potato mixture and mix until well combined.
5. Spoon batter into the prepared muffin pan.
6. Select bake mode. Set the temperature to 350 F and the timer for 25 minutes. Press start.
7. Let the air fryer preheat then insert the pizza rack into shelf position 5.
8. Place muffin pan on the pizza rack and cook.
9. Serve and enjoy.

Nutritional Value (Amount per Serving):

- Calories 108
- Fat 0.5 g
- Carbohydrates 22.9 g
- Sugar 0.9 g
- Protein 2.6 g
- Cholesterol 1 mg

Broccoli Egg Breakfast Bake

Preparation Time: 10 minutes
Cooking Time: 30 minutes
Serve: 12
Ingredients:

- 12 eggs
- 2 cups broccoli florets, chopped
- 1 onion, diced

- 1 1/2 cup mozzarella cheese, shredded
- 1 cup milk
- Pepper
- Salt

Directions:

1. Spray a 9*13-inch baking dish with cooking spray and set aside.
2. In a large bowl, mix eggs, pepper, milk, and salt.
3. Add cheese, broccoli, and onion and mix well.
4. Pour egg mixture into the prepared baking dish.
5. Select bake mode. Set the temperature to 390 F and the timer for 30 minutes. Press start.
6. Let the air fryer preheat then insert the pizza rack into shelf position 5.
7. Place baking dish on the pizza rack and cook.
8. Slice and serve.

Nutritional Value (Amount per Serving):

- Calories 92
- Fat 5.5 g
- Carbohydrates 3.4 g
- Sugar 1.9 g
- Protein 7.7 g
- Cholesterol 167 mg

Vegetable Frittata

Preparation Time: 10 minutes
Cooking Time: 35 minutes
Serve: 6

Ingredients:

- 10 eggs
- 1 sweet potato, diced
- 2 cups broccoli, chopped
- 1 tbsp olive oil
- 1/4 cup feta cheese, crumbled
- 1 onion, diced
- Pepper
- Salt

Directions:

1. Spray a baking dish with cooking spray and set aside.
2. Heat oil in a pan over medium heat.
3. Add sweet potato, broccoli, and onion and cook for 15 minutes or until sweet potato is tender.
4. In a large bowl, whisk eggs with pepper and salt.
5. Transfer cooked vegetables into the baking dish.
6. Pour egg mixture over vegetables. Sprinkle with feta cheese.

7. Select bake mode. Set the temperature to 390 F and the timer for 20 minutes. Press start.
8. Let the air fryer preheat then insert the pizza rack into shelf position 5.
9. Place baking dish on the pizza rack and cook.
10. Slice and serve.

Nutritional Value (Amount per Serving):

- Calories 176
- Fat 11.1 g
- Carbohydrates 8.5 g
- Sugar 3.4 g
- Protein 11.5 g
- Cholesterol 278 mg

Baked Breakfast Casserole

Preparation Time: 10 minutes
Cooking Time: 60 minutes
Serve: 6

Ingredients:

- 4 eggs
- 1 1/2 cup mozzarella cheese, shredded
- 5 bread slices, cut into cubes
- 2 cups of milk
- Pepper
- Salt

Directions:

1. Spray 1 1/2-quart baking dish with cooking spray and set aside.
2. Layer bread cubes and shredded cheese alternately in the prepared baking dish.
3. In a bowl, whisk eggs with milk, pepper, and salt and pour over the bread mixture.
4. Place a baking dish in the refrigerator overnight.
5. Select bake mode. Set the temperature to 350 F and the timer for 60 minutes. Press start.
6. Let the air fryer preheat then insert the pizza rack into shelf position 5.
7. Place baking dish on the pizza rack and cook.
8. Slice and serve.

Nutritional Value (Amount per Serving):

- Calories 123
- Fat 6.1 g
- Carbohydrates 8.3 g
- Sugar 4.2 g
- Protein 8.9 g
- Cholesterol 120 mg

Berry Baked Oatmeal

Preparation Time: 10 minutes
Cooking Time: 20 minutes
Serve: 4

Ingredients:

- 1 egg
- 2 cups old fashioned oats
- 1 cup blueberries
- 1 cup strawberries, sliced
- 1 1/2 tsp baking powder
- 1/4 cup maple syrup
- 1 1/2 cups milk
- 1/2 tsp salt

Directions:

1. Spray a baking dish with cooking spray and set aside.
2. In a mixing bowl, mix oats, salt, and baking powder.
3. Add vanilla, egg, maple syrup, and milk and stir well.
4. Add berries and stir well.
5. Pour mixture into the baking dish.
6. Select bake mode. Set the temperature to 375 F and the timer for 20 minutes. Press start.
7. Let the air fryer preheat then insert the pizza rack into shelf position 5.
8. Place baking dish on the pizza rack and cook.
9. Serve and enjoy.

Nutritional Value (Amount per Serving):

- Calories 459
- Fat 8.4 g
- Carbohydrates 80.4 g
- Sugar 23.4 g
- Protein 14.9 g
- Cholesterol 48 mg

Chapter 3: Poultry

Ranch Chicken Wings

Preparation Time: 10 minutes
Cooking Time: 25 minutes
Serve: 2

Ingredients:

- 1 lb chicken wings
- 2 tbsp butter, melted
- 1 1/2 tbsp ranch seasoning
- 1 tbsp garlic, minced

Directions:

1. In a bowl, mix butter, garlic, and ranch seasoning.
2. Add chicken wings and toss to coat.
3. Cover bowl and place in the refrigerator overnight.
4. Arrange marinated chicken wings in a crispier tray.
5. Place the drip tray below the bottom of the air fryer.
6. Insert the crispier tray into shelf position 4.
7. Select air fry mode. Set the temperature to 360 F and the timer for 25 minutes. Press start.
8. Turn chicken wings halfway through.
9. Serve and enjoy.

Nutritional Value (Amount per Serving):

- Calories 561
- Fat 28.4 g
- Carbohydrates 1.4 g
- Sugar 0.1 g
- Protein 66 g
- Cholesterol 232 mg

Lemon Pepper Chicken

Preparation Time: 10 minutes
Cooking Time: 15 minutes
Serve: 6

Ingredients:

- 6 chicken thighs, skinless & boneless
- 1/2 tbsp lemon pepper seasoning
- 1 1/2 tbsp fresh lemon juice
- 1/2 tsp garlic powder
- 1/2 tsp Italian seasoning
- 1/2 tsp paprika
- Pepper
- Salt

Directions:

1. Add chicken thighs into the bowl.
2. Add remaining ingredients and coat well.
3. Place chicken thighs in a crispier tray.
4. Place the drip tray below the bottom of the air fryer.
5. Insert the crispier tray into shelf position 4.
6. Select air fry mode. Set the temperature to 360 F and the timer for 15 minutes. Press start.
7. Serve and enjoy.

Nutritional Value (Amount per Serving):

- Calories 282
- Fat 11 g
- Carbohydrates 0.7 g
- Sugar 0.2 g
- Protein 42.4 g
- Cholesterol 130 mg

Jerk Wings

Preparation Time: 10 minutes
Cooking Time: 20 minutes
Serve: 2
Ingredients:

- 1 lb chicken wings
- 1 tbsp jerk seasoning
- 1 tsp olive oil
- 1 tbsp cornstarch
- Pepper
- Salt

Directions:

1. In a bowl, add chicken wings.
2. Add remaining ingredients on top of chicken wings and toss well.
3. Add chicken wings in a crispier tray.
4. Place the drip tray below the bottom of the air fryer.
5. Insert the crispier tray into shelf position 4.
6. Select air fry mode. Set the temperature to 380 F and the timer for 20 minutes. Press start.
7. Turn chicken wings halfway through.
8. Serve and enjoy.

Nutritional Value (Amount per Serving):

- Calories 466
- Fat 19.1 g
- Carbohydrates 3.7 g
- Sugar 0 g
- Protein 65.6 g
- Cholesterol 202 mg

Greek Chicken Breast

Preparation Time: 10 minutes
Cooking Time: 25 minutes
Serve: 4
Ingredients:

- 4 chicken breasts, skinless & boneless
- 1 tbsp olive oil
- For rub:
- 1 tsp oregano
- 1 tsp thyme
- 1 tsp parsley
- 1 tsp onion powder
- 1 tsp basil
- Pepper
- Salt

Directions:

1. Brush chicken breast with oil.
2. In a small bowl, mix all rub ingredients and rub all over chicken breasts.
3. Place chicken in a crispier tray.
4. Place the drip tray below the bottom of the air fryer.
5. Insert the crispier tray into shelf position 4.
6. Select air fry mode. Set the temperature to 390 F and the timer for 25 minutes. Press start.
7. Turn chicken halfway through.
8. Serve and enjoy.

Nutritional Value (Amount per Serving):

- Calories 312
- Fat 14.4 g
- Carbohydrates 0.9 g
- Sugar 0.2 g
- Protein 42.4 g
- Cholesterol 130 mg

Tasty Chicken Tenders

Preparation Time: 10 minutes
Cooking Time: 16 minutes
Serve: 4
Ingredients:

- 1 lb chicken tenders
- For rub:
- 1/2 tbsp dried thyme
- 1 tbsp garlic powder
- 1 tbsp paprika
- 1/2 tbsp onion powder

- 1/2 tsp cayenne pepper
- Pepper
- Salt

Directions:
1. In a bowl, add all rub ingredients and mix well.
2. Add chicken tenders into the bowl and coat well.
3. Place chicken tenders in a crispier tray.
4. Place the drip tray below the bottom of the air fryer.
5. Insert the crispier tray into shelf position 4.
6. Select air fry mode. Set the temperature to 370 F and the timer for 16 minutes. Press start.
7. Turn chicken tenders halfway through.
8. Serve and enjoy.

Nutritional Value (Amount per Serving):
- Calories 232
- Fat 8.7 g
- Carbohydrates 3.6 g
- Sugar 1 g
- Protein 33.6 g
- Cholesterol 101 mg

Meatballs

Preparation Time: 10 minutes
Cooking Time: 20 minutes
Serve: 4
Ingredients:
- 1 lb ground turkey
- 2 garlic cloves, minced
- 1/4 cup basil, chopped
- 3 tbsp scallions, chopped
- 1 egg, lightly beaten
- 1/2 cup almond flour
- 1/2 tsp red pepper, crushed
- 1 tbsp lemongrass, chopped
- 1 1/2 tbsp fish sauce

Directions:
1. Add all ingredients into a large bowl and mix until well combined.
2. Make balls from the meat mixture and place them in a crispier tray.
3. Place the drip tray below the bottom of the air fryer.
4. Insert the crispier tray into shelf position 4.
5. Select air fry mode. Set the temperature to 380 F and the timer for 20 minutes. Press start.
6. Turn meatballs halfway through.
7. Serve and enjoy.

Nutritional Value (Amount per Serving):

- Calories 333
- Fat 20.3 g
- Carbohydrates 5.6 g
- Sugar 1.2 g
- Protein 36.2 g
- Cholesterol 157 mg

Flavors Chicken Fajita

Preparation Time: 10 minutes
Cooking Time: 16 minutes
Serve: 4
Ingredients:

- 1 lb chicken breast, skinless, boneless, and sliced
- 1/8 tsp cayenne
- 2 tsp olive oil
- 1 onion, sliced
- 2 bell peppers, sliced
- 1 tsp cumin
- 2 tsp chili powder
- 1/2 tsp pepper
- 1 tsp salt

Directions:

1. Add chicken and remaining ingredients into the mixing bowl and toss well.
2. Transfer chicken mixture to the crispier tray.
3. Place the drip tray below the bottom of the air fryer.
4. Insert the crispier tray into shelf position 4.
5. Select air fry mode. Set the temperature to 360 F and the timer for 16 minutes. Press start.
6. Stir chicken mixture halfway through.
7. Serve and enjoy.

Nutritional Value (Amount per Serving):

- Calories 186
- Fat 5.7 g
- Carbohydrates 8.2 g
- Sugar 4.3 g
- Protein 25.2 g
- Cholesterol 73 mg

Easy Air Fryer Chicken

Preparation Time: 10 minutes
Cooking Time: 18 minutes
Serve: 2
Ingredients:

- 2 chicken breasts, skinless and boneless
- 2 tsp olive oil
- 1 tsp poultry seasoning

Directions:

1. Brush chicken breasts with oil and rub with poultry seasoning.
2. Place chicken in a crispier tray.
3. Place the drip tray below the bottom of the air fryer.
4. Insert the crispier tray into shelf position 4.
5. Select air fry mode. Set the temperature to 350 F and the timer for 18 minutes. Press start.
6. Turn chicken halfway through.
7. Serve and enjoy.

Nutritional Value (Amount per Serving):

- Calories 320
- Fat 15.6 g
- Carbohydrates 0.5 g
- Sugar 0 g
- Protein 42.3 g
- Cholesterol 130 mg

Turkey Patties

Preparation Time: 10 minutes
Cooking Time: 22 minutes
Serve: 4
Ingredients:

- 1 lb ground turkey
- 1 tbsp garlic paste
- 4 oz goat cheese, crumbled
- 1 1/4 cup spinach, chopped
- 1 tsp Italian seasoning
- 1 tbsp olive oil
- Pepper
- Salt

Directions:

1. Add all ingredients into the bowl and mix until well combined.
2. Make patties from the mixture and place them in the crisper tray.
3. Place the drip tray below the bottom of the air fryer.
4. Insert the crispier tray into shelf position 4.
5. Select air fry mode. Set the temperature to 390s F and the timer for 22 minutes. Press start.
6. Turn patties halfway through.
7. Serve and enjoy.

Nutritional Value (Amount per Serving):

- Calories 388
- Fat 26.4 g

- Carbohydrates 1.8 g
- Sugar 0.8 g
- Protein 40.1 g
- Cholesterol 146 mg

Tasty Chicken Burger Patties

Preparation Time: 10 minutes
Cooking Time: 18 minutes
Serve: 4
Ingredients:
- 1 lb ground chicken
- 3.5 oz breadcrumbs
- 1 tbsp oregano
- 1.5 oz mozzarella cheese, shredded
- Pepper
- Salt

Directions:
1. Add all ingredients into the bowl and mix until well combined.
2. Make patties from the meat mixture and place them in the crisper tray.
3. Place the drip tray below the bottom of the air fryer.
4. Insert the crispier tray into shelf position 4.
5. Select air fry mode. Set the temperature to 360 F and the timer for 18 minutes. Press start.
6. Turn patties halfway through.
7. Serve and enjoy.

Nutritional Value (Amount per Serving):
- Calories 347
- Fat 11.7 g
- Carbohydrates 19 g
- Sugar 1.6 g
- Protein 39.2 g
- Cholesterol 107 mg

Meatballs

Preparation Time: 10 minutes
Cooking Time: 10 minutes
Serve: 4
Ingredients:
- 1 egg
- 1 lb ground chicken
- 1/2 cup breadcrumbs
- 1/2 cup parmesan cheese, shredded
- 1/2 tsp onion powder
- Pepper
- Salt

Directions:

1. Add all ingredients into the bowl and mix until well combined.
2. Make balls from the meat mixture and place them in a crispier tray.
3. Place the drip tray below the bottom of the air fryer.
4. Insert the crispier tray into shelf position 4.
5. Select air fry mode. Set the temperature to 370 F and the timer for 10 minutes. Press start.
6. Turn meatballs halfway through.
7. Serve and enjoy.

Nutritional Value (Amount per Serving):

- Calories 322
- Fat 12.6 g
- Carbohydrates 10.5 g
- Sugar 1 g
- Protein 39.6 g
- Cholesterol 150 mg

Greek Herb Chicken Breasts

Preparation Time: 10 minutes
Cooking Time: 10 minutes
Serve: 2

Ingredients:

- 2 chicken breasts, boneless and skinless
- 1 tsp dried oregano
- 1 tsp dried basil
- 2 tsp garlic, minced
- 1 tsp dried thyme
- Pepper
- Salt

Directions:

1. In a small bowl, mix garlic, thyme, oregano, basil, pepper, and salt and rub all over the chicken.
2. Place chicken in a crispier tray.
3. Place the drip tray below the bottom of the air fryer.
4. Insert the crispier tray into shelf position 4.
5. Select air fry mode. Set the temperature to 400 F and the timer for 10 minutes. Press start.
6. Serve and enjoy.

Nutritional Value (Amount per Serving):

- Calories 285
- Fat 11 g
- Carbohydrates 1.8 g
- Sugar 0.1 g
- Protein 42.6 g
- Cholesterol 130 mg

Meatballs

Preparation Time: 10 minutes
Cooking Time: 10 minutes
Serve: 4
Ingredients:

- 1 lb ground turkey
- 1 egg, lightly beaten
- 1/2 cup breadcrumbs
- 1 tbsp soy sauce
- 1/4 cup fresh parsley, chopped
- Pepper
- Salt

Directions:

1. Add all ingredients into the bowl and mix until well combined.
2. Make balls from the meat mixture and place them in a crispier tray.
3. Place the drip tray below the bottom of the air fryer.
4. Insert the crispier tray into shelf position 4.
5. Select air fry mode. Set the temperature to 400 F and the timer for 10 minutes. Press start.
6. Turn meatballs halfway through.
7. Serve and enjoy.

Nutritional Value (Amount per Serving):

- Calories 294
- Fat 14.3 g
- Carbohydrates 10.4 g
- Sugar 1 g
- Protein 34.6 g
- Cholesterol 157 mg

Tasty Chicken Fritters

Preparation Time: 10 minutes
Cooking Time: 25 minutes
Serve: 4
Ingredients:

- 1 lb ground chicken
- 1 tsp garlic, minced
- 1 egg, lightly beaten
- 1 1/2 cups mozzarella cheese, shredded
- 1/2 cup onion, chopped
- 2 cups broccoli, chopped
- 3/4 cup breadcrumbs
- Pepper
- Salt

Directions:

1. Add all ingredients into the bowl and mix until well combined.
2. Make patties from the meat mixture and place them in the crisper tray.
3. Place the drip tray below the bottom of the air fryer.
4. Insert the crispier tray into shelf position 4.
5. Select air fry mode. Set the temperature to 380 F and the timer for 25 minutes. Press start.
6. Turn patties halfway through.
7. Serve and enjoy.

Nutritional Value (Amount per Serving):
- Calories 364
- Fat 12.6 g
- Carbohydrates 19.7 g
- Sugar 2.7 g
- Protein 41.4 g
- Cholesterol 147 mg

Delicious Chicken Thighs

Preparation Time: 10 minutes
Cooking Time: 35 minutes
Serve: 6
Ingredients:
- 6 chicken thighs
- 1 tbsp olive oil
- For rub:
- 1/2 tsp pepper
- 1 tsp garlic powder
- 1 tsp onion powder
- 1/2 tsp basil
- 1/2 tsp oregano
- 1/2 tsp salt

Directions:
1. Brush chicken thighs with oil.
2. In a small bowl, mix rub ingredients and rub all over the chicken.
3. Arrange chicken on a baking sheet.
4. Select bake mode. Set the temperature to 390 F and the timer for 35 minutes. Press start.
5. Let the air fryer preheat then insert the pizza rack into shelf position 5.
6. Place baking sheet on the pizza rack and cook.
7. Serve and enjoy.

Nutritional Value (Amount per Serving):
- Calories 301
- Fat 13.2 g
- Carbohydrates 0.9 g
- Sugar 0.3 g
- Protein 42.4 g
- Cholesterol 130 mg

Marinated Greek Chicken

Preparation Time: 10 minutes
Cooking Time: 30 minutes
Serve: 4
Ingredients:

- 1 lb chicken breasts, skinless & boneless
- For marinade:
- 3 garlic cloves, minced
- 1 tbsp lime juice
- 1/2 tsp dill
- 1 tsp onion powder
- 1/4 tsp basil
- 1/4 tsp oregano
- 3 tbsp olive oil
- 1/4 tsp pepper
- 1/2 tsp salt

Directions:

1. Add all marinade ingredients into the bowl and mix well.
2. Add chicken into the marinade and coat well.
3. Cover and place in the refrigerator overnight.
4. Arrange marinated chicken on a baking sheet.
5. Select bake mode. Set the temperature to 390 F and the timer for 30 minutes. Press start.
6. Let the air fryer preheat then insert the pizza rack into shelf position 5.
7. Place baking sheet on the pizza rack and cook.
8. Serve and enjoy.

Nutritional Value (Amount per Serving):

- Calories 313
- Fat 19 g
- Carbohydrates 1.5 g
- Sugar 0.3 g
- Protein 33.1 g
- Cholesterol 101 mg

Crispy Chicken Breast

Preparation Time: 10 minutes
Cooking Time: 35 minutes
Serve: 4
Ingredients:

- 4 chicken breasts, skinless and boneless
- 1 cup cracker crumbs
- 2 eggs, lightly beaten
- 1/2 cup butter, cut into pieces
- Pepper

- Salt

Directions:

1. Add cracker crumbs and eggs in 2 separate shallow dishes.
2. Mix cracker crumbs with pepper and salt.
3. Dip chicken in the eggs and then coat with cracker crumb.
4. Arrange coated chicken in a baking dish.
5. Spread butter pieces on top of the chicken.
6. Select bake mode. Set the temperature to 375 F and the timer for 35 minutes. Press start.
7. Let the air fryer preheat then insert the pizza rack into shelf position 5.
8. Place baking dish on the pizza rack and cook.
9. Serve and enjoy.

Nutritional Value (Amount per Serving):

- Calories 590
- Fat 40 g
- Carbohydrates 9.7 g
- Sugar 0.5 g
- Protein 46.4 g
- Cholesterol 273 mg

Ranch Chicken Broccoli

Preparation Time: 10 minutes
Cooking Time: 30 minutes
Serve: 4

Ingredients:

- 4 chicken breasts, skinless and boneless
- 4 bacon slices, cooked and chopped
- 2 cups broccoli florets, blanched and chopped
- 1/3 cup mozzarella cheese, shredded
- 1 cup cheddar cheese, shredded
- 1/2 cup ranch dressing

Directions:

1. Add chicken in a 13*9-inch casserole dish. Top with bacon and broccoli.
2. Pour ranch dressing over chicken and top with mozzarella cheese and cheddar cheese.
3. Select bake mode. Set the temperature to 375 F and the timer for 30 minutes. Press start.
4. Let the air fryer preheat then insert the pizza rack into shelf position 5.
5. Place baking dish on the pizza rack and cook.

6. Serve and enjoy.

Nutritional Value (Amount per Serving):
- Calories 525
- Fat 28.8 g
- Carbohydrates 5.4 g
- Sugar 1.7 g
- Protein 58.6 g
- Cholesterol 182 mg

Creamy Chicken

Preparation Time: 10 minutes
Cooking Time: 45 minutes
Serve: 4

Ingredients:
- 4 chicken breasts, skinless, boneless & cut into chunks
- 1 cup parmesan cheese, shredded
- 1 cup mayonnaise
- 1 tsp garlic powder
- Pepper
- Salt

Directions:
1. Add chicken into the bowl. Add buttermilk and soak overnight.
2. Add marinated chicken into the 9*13-inch baking dish.
3. Mix together mayonnaise, garlic powder, 1/2 cup parmesan cheese, pepper, and salt and pour over chicken.
4. Sprinkle remaining cheese on top of the chicken.
5. Select bake mode. Set the temperature to 375 F and the timer for 45 minutes. Press start.
6. Let the air fryer preheat then insert the pizza rack into shelf position 5.
7. Place baking dish on the pizza rack and cook.
8. Serve and enjoy.

Nutritional Value (Amount per Serving):
- Calories 581
- Fat 35.3 g
- Carbohydrates 15.4 g
- Sugar 3.9 g
- Protein 50.1 g
- Cholesterol 161 mg

Rosemary Chicken & Potatoes

Preparation Time: 10 minutes
Cooking Time: 60 minutes
Serve: 5

Ingredients:

- 5 chicken thighs
- 1 lemon juice
- 2 lbs potatoes, cut into chunks
- 4 garlic cloves, minced
- 1/2 cup olive oil
- 1 tbsp fresh rosemary, chopped
- 1 tsp dried oregano
- Pepper
- Salt

Directions:

1. In a large bowl, add chicken and remaining ingredients and mix well.
2. Place chicken in the baking dish and spread potatoes around the chicken.
3. Select bake mode. Set the temperature to 375 F and the timer for 60 minutes. Press start.
4. Let the air fryer preheat then insert the pizza rack into shelf position 5.
5. Place baking dish on the pizza rack and cook.
6. Serve and enjoy.

Nutritional Value (Amount per Serving):

- Calories 584
- Fat 21.4 g
- Carbohydrates 30.1 g
- Sugar 2.3 g
- Protein 45.6 g
- Cholesterol 130 mg

Parmesan Chicken Breasts

Preparation Time: 10 minutes
Cooking Time: 35 minutes
Serve: 4
Ingredients:

- 4 chicken breasts
- 1 cup breadcrumbs
- 1/4 cup olive oil
- 1 cup parmesan cheese, shredded
- Pepper
- Salt

Directions:

1. Season chicken with pepper and salt and brush with olive oil.
2. In a shallow dish, mix parmesan cheese and breadcrumbs.
3. Coat chicken with parmesan and breadcrumb mixture and place in the baking dish.
4. Select bake mode. Set the temperature to 350 F and the timer for 35 minutes. Press start.
5. Let the air fryer preheat then insert the pizza rack into shelf position 5.
6. Place baking dish on the pizza rack and cook.
7. Serve and enjoy.

Nutritional Value (Amount per Serving):

- Calories 508
- Fat 23.3 g
- Carbohydrates 20.3 g
- Sugar 1.7 g
- Protein 53.1 g
- Cholesterol 128 mg

BBQ Chicken Wings

Preparation Time: 10 minutes
Cooking Time: 45 minutes
Serve: 6
Ingredients:

- 3 lbs chicken wings
- 1/2 cup BBQ spice rub
- 2 tbsp olive oil

Directions:

1. Brush chicken wings with oil and place in a bowl.
2. Add BBQ spice over chicken wings and toss well.
3. Arrange chicken wings on a baking sheet.
4. Select bake mode. Set the temperature to 390 F and the timer for 45 minutes. Press start.
5. Let the air fryer preheat then insert the pizza rack into shelf position 5.
6. Place baking sheet on the pizza rack and cook.
7. Serve and enjoy.

Nutritional Value (Amount per Serving):

- Calories 483
- Fat 22.2 g
- Carbohydrates 1.5 g
- Sugar 0.2 g
- Protein 65.8 g
- Cholesterol 202 mg

Lemon Garlic Chicken

Preparation Time: 10 minutes
Cooking Time: 6 hours
Serve: 4
Ingredients:

- 4 chicken breasts, skinless & boneless
- 1/4 cup lemon juice
- 2 tsp dried oregano
- 3 tbsp parsley, chopped
- 1 cup chicken broth
- 1 tbsp lemon zest
- 1 tbsp garlic, minced

- 1 tsp kosher salt

Directions:

1. Add all ingredients into the dutch oven and mix well.
2. Cover the dutch oven with a lid.
3. Insert the pizza rack into shelf position 6.
4. Place dutch oven on pizza rack.
5. Select a slow cook mode. Set the temperature to 225 F and the timer for 6 hours. Press start.
6. Serve and enjoy.

Nutritional Value (Amount per Serving):

- Calories 298
- Fat 11.4 g
- Carbohydrates 2.2 g
- Sugar 0.6 g
- Protein 43.9 g
- Cholesterol 130 mg

Tasty Smothered Chicken

Preparation Time: 10 minutes
Cooking Time: 55 minutes
Serve: 4
Ingredients:

- 4 chicken breasts
- 1 tbsp cornstarch
- 3/4 cup parmesan cheese, grated
- 1 cup sour cream
- 4 mozzarella cheese slices
- 1/2 tsp garlic powder
- 1 tsp dried basil
- 1 tsp dried oregano
- 1/4 tsp pepper
- 1/2 tsp salt

Directions:

1. Place chicken breasts into the baking dish and top with mozzarella cheese slices.
2. In a bowl, mix sour cream, oregano, basil, garlic powder, pepper, parmesan cheese, cornstarch, and salt.
3. Pour cream mixture over chicken.
4. Select bake mode. Set the temperature to 375 F and the timer for 55 minutes. Press start.
5. Let the air fryer preheat then insert the pizza rack into shelf position 5.
6. Place baking dish on the pizza rack and cook.
7. Serve and enjoy.

Nutritional Value (Amount per Serving):

- Calories 545
- Fat 31.5 g

- Carbohydrates 6.5 g
- Sugar 0.2 g
- Protein 57.6 g
- Cholesterol 182 mg

Baked Balsamic Chicken

Preparation Time: 10 minutes
Cooking Time: 25 minutes
Serve: 4
Ingredients:

- 4 chicken breasts, boneless & skinless
- 2 tbsp soy sauce
- 1/4 cup olive oil
- 1/4 tsp pepper
- 2 tsp dried oregano
- 2 garlic clove, minced
- 1/2 cup balsamic vinegar
- 1/4 tsp salt

Directions:

1. Place chicken into the baking dish.
2. Mix remaining ingredients and pour over chicken.
3. Select bake mode. Set the temperature to 400 F and the timer for 25 minutes. Press start.
4. Let the air fryer preheat then insert the pizza rack into shelf position 5.
5. Place baking dish on the pizza rack and cook.
6. Serve and enjoy.

Nutritional Value (Amount per Serving):

- Calories 401
- Fat 23.5 g
- Carbohydrates 2 g
- Sugar 0.3 g
- Protein 42.9 g
- Cholesterol 130 mg

Chapter 4: Beef, Pork & Lamb

Slow Cook Flank Steak

Preparation Time: 10 minutes
Cooking Time: 9 hours
Serve: 6
Ingredients:

- 1 1/2 lbs flank steak
- 2 bell pepper, sliced
- 1 1/2 tsp chili powder
- 15 oz salsa
- 3 garlic cloves, minced
- 1 onion, chopped
- 1/4 tsp pepper
- 1/2 tsp salt

Directions:

1. Add all ingredients into the large zip-lock bag and mix well.
2. Place a zip-lock bag into the fridge overnight.
3. Add marinated steak into the dutch oven and cover with a lid.
4. Insert the pizza rack into shelf position 6.
5. Place dutch oven on pizza rack.
6. Select a slow cook mode. Set the temperature to 225 F and the timer for 9 hours. Press start.
7. Slice and serve.

Nutritional Value (Amount per Serving):

- Calories 264
- Fat 9.8 g
- Carbohydrates 10.1 g
- Sugar 5 g
- Protein 33.4 g
- Cholesterol 62 mg

Flavorful Steak Fajitas

Preparation Time: 10 minutes
Cooking Time: 4 hours
Serve: 6
Ingredients:

- 2 lbs beef, sliced
- 2 bell pepper, sliced
- 2 tbsp fajita seasoning
- 20 oz salsa
- 1 onion, sliced

Directions:

1. Add salsa into the dutch oven.

2. Add meat, bell peppers, onion, and fajita seasoning. Stir well.
3. Cover the dutch oven with a lid.
4. Insert the pizza rack into shelf position 6.
5. Place dutch oven on pizza rack.
6. Select a slow cook mode. Set the temperature to 275 F and the timer for 4 hours. Press start.
7. Serve and enjoy.

Nutritional Value (Amount per Serving):
- Calories 337
- Fat 9.7 g
- Carbohydrates 12.7 g
- Sugar 5.7 g
- Protein 47.9 g
- Cholesterol 135 mg

Curried Pork Chops

Preparation Time: 10 minutes
Cooking Time: 6 hours
Serve: 8
Ingredients:
- 2 lbs pork chops
- 1 tbsp dried rosemary
- 1/4 cup extra-virgin olive oil
- 1 tbsp ground cumin
- 1 tbsp fennel seeds
- 1 tbsp fresh chives, chopped
- 1 tbsp curry powder
- 1 tbsp dried thyme
- 1 tsp salt

Directions:
1. In a small bowl, mix cumin, rosemary, 2 tbsp oil, fennel seeds, chives, curry powder, thyme, and salt and rub over pork chops.
2. Place pork chops into the dutch oven.
3. Pour remaining oil over pork chops.
4. Cover the dutch oven with a lid.
5. Insert the pizza rack into shelf position 6.
6. Place dutch oven on pizza rack.
7. Select a slow cook mode. Set the temperature to 225 F and the timer for 6 hours. Press start.
8. Serve and enjoy.

Nutritional Value (Amount per Serving):
- Calories 427
- Fat 35 g
- Carbohydrates 1.7 g
- Sugar 0.1 g

- Protein 25.9 g
- Cholesterol 98 mg

Salsa Pork Chops

Preparation Time: 10 minutes
Cooking Time: 3 hours
Serve: 8
Ingredients:

- 8 pork chops, bone-in
- 3 tbsp extra-virgin olive oil
- 1 tsp garlic powder
- 1/2 tsp ground cumin
- 1/4 cup fresh lime juice
- 1/2 cup salsa
- Pepper
- Salt

Directions:

1. Heat in a pan over medium-high heat.
2. Add pork chops in a pan and cook until browned.
3. Place pork chops into the dutch oven.
4. Pour remaining ingredients over pork chops.
5. Cover the dutch oven with a lid.
6. Insert the pizza rack into shelf position 6.
7. Place dutch oven on pizza rack.
8. Select a slow cook mode. Set the temperature to 275 F and the timer for 3 hours. Press start.
9. Serve and enjoy.

Nutritional Value (Amount per Serving):

- Calories 307
- Fat 25.2 g
- Carbohydrates 1.5 g
- Sugar 0.6 g
- Protein 18.3 g
- Cholesterol 69 mg

Delicious Carnitas

Preparation Time: 10 minutes
Cooking Time: 8 hours
Serve: 12
Ingredients:

- 3 lbs pork butt roast
- 1 tbsp whole juniper berries
- 1/2 tsp pepper
- 2 tbsp olive oil
- 1/2 cup water
- 1/2 tsp dried thyme

- 3 bay leaves
- 1 tbsp salt

Directions:

1. Heat olive oil in a pot over high heat.
2. Season pork butt with pepper and salt.
3. Add pork into the pot and sear for 4 minutes on each side.
4. Transfer pork into the dutch oven along with remaining ingredients.
5. Cover the dutch oven with a lid.
6. Insert the pizza rack into shelf position 6.
7. Place dutch oven on pizza rack.
8. Select a slow cook mode. Set the temperature to 225 F and the timer for 8 hours. Press start.
9. Once done, remove pork from the dutch oven and shred using the fork.
10. Serve and enjoy.

Nutritional Value (Amount per Serving):

- Calories 232
- Sugar 0 g
- Fat 16.4 g
- Protein 20.2 g
- Carbohydrates 0.2 g
- Cholesterol 70 mg

Shredded Beef

Preparation Time: 10 minutes
Cooking Time: 8 hours
Serve: 6

Ingredients:

- 3 lbs rump roast
- 1 1/3 cups beef broth
- 1 tbsp cumin
- 1 onion, quartered
- 2/3 cup tomato sauce
- 2 tbsp garlic, minced
- 10 oz can green enchilada sauce
- Salt

Directions:

1. Place roast in the dutch oven. Pour remaining ingredients over roast.
2. Cover the dutch oven with a lid.
3. Insert the pizza rack into shelf position 6.
4. Place dutch oven on pizza rack.
5. Select a slow cook mode. Set the temperature to 225 F and the timer for 8 hours. Press start.
6. Remove roast from dutch oven and shred using a fork.
7. Serve and enjoy.

Nutritional Value (Amount per Serving):

- Calories 488
- Fat 15.4 g
- Carbohydrates 13.3 g
- Sugar 2.5 g
- Protein 74.1 g
- Cholesterol 5 mg

Meatballs

Preparation Time: 10 minutes
Cooking Time: 15 minutes
Serve: 6
Ingredients:

- 1 egg
- 20 oz ground beef
- 2 tbsp parsley, chopped
- 1/2 cup parmesan cheese, grated
- 8 tbsp almond milk
- 6 garlic cloves, minced
- 2 tbsp olive oil
- 3/4 cups almond meal
- 2 tbsp basil, chopped
- 1 tsp black pepper
- 1 tsp salt

Directions:

1. Add all ingredients except oil into the mixing bowl and mix until well combined.
2. Make balls from the meat mixture.
3. Heat oil in a pan over medium heat.
4. Add meatballs in hot oil and cook until just browned.
5. Transfer meatballs into the baking dish.
6. Select bake mode. Set the temperature to 350 F and the timer for 10 minutes. Press start.
7. Let the air fryer preheat then insert the pizza rack into shelf position 5.
8. Place baking dish on the pizza rack and cook.
9. Serve and enjoy.

Nutritional Value (Amount per Serving):

- Calories 371
- Fat 23.7 g
- Carbohydrates 5.3 g
- Sugar 1.3 g
- Protein 35.3 g
- Cholesterol 117 mg

Tasty Beef Fajitas

Preparation Time: 10 minutes
Cooking Time: 8 minutes

Serve: 4

Ingredients:

- 1 lb beef flank steak, sliced
- 1/2 tbsp chili powder
- 3 tbsp olive oil
- 2 bell peppers, sliced
- 1 tsp garlic powder
- 1 tsp paprika
- 1 1/2 tsp cumin
- Pepper
- Salt

Directions:

1. In a bowl, toss sliced steak with remaining ingredients.
2. Add meat mixture to the crispier tray.
3. Place the drip tray below the bottom of the air fryer.
4. Insert the crispier tray into shelf position 4.
5. Select air fry mode. Set the temperature to 390 F and the timer for 8 minutes. Press start.
6. Stir the mixture after 3 minutes.
7. Serve and enjoy.

Nutritional Value (Amount per Serving):

- Calories 330
- Fat 18.1 g
- Carbohydrates 6.2 g
- Sugar 3.3 g
- Protein 35.5 g
- Cholesterol 101 mg

Meatballs

Preparation Time: 10 minutes
Cooking Time: 14 minutes
Serve: 4

Ingredients:

- 1 lb ground beef
- 1/4 cup breadcrumbs
- 1/2 onion, diced
- 1 tsp garlic powder
- 1 egg, lightly beaten
- Pepper
- Salt

Directions:

1. Add all ingredients into the bowl and mix until well combined.
2. Make balls from the meat mixture and place them in a crispier tray.
3. Place the drip tray below the bottom of the air fryer.
4. Insert the crispier tray into shelf position 4.

5. Select air fry mode. Set the temperature to 390 F and the timer for 14 minutes. Press start.
6. Turn meatballs halfway through.
7. Serve and enjoy.

Nutritional Value (Amount per Serving):

- Calories 261
- Fat 8.5 g
- Carbohydrates 6.8 g
- Sugar 1.3 g
- Protein 37 g
- Cholesterol 142 mg

Air Fryer Steak

Preparation Time: 10 minutes
Cooking Time: 18 minutes
Serve: 2

Ingredients:

- 12 oz steaks
- 1/4 tsp onion powder
- 1 tsp olive oil
- 1/2 tsp garlic powder
- Pepper
- Salt

Directions:

1. Brush steaks with oil and season with garlic powder, onion powder, pepper, and salt.
2. Place steaks in a crispier tray.
3. Place the drip tray below the bottom of the air fryer.
4. Insert the crispier tray into shelf position 4.
5. Select air fry mode. Set the temperature to 400 F and the timer for 18 minutes. Press start.
6. Turn steak halfway through.
7. Serve and enjoy.

Nutritional Value (Amount per Serving):

- Calories 362
- Fat 10.9 g
- Carbohydrates 0.8 g
- Sugar 0.3 g
- Protein 61.6 g
- Cholesterol 153 mg

Steak & Mushrooms

Preparation Time: 10 minutes
Cooking Time: 18 minutes

Serve: 4

Ingredients:

- 1 lb steaks, cut into 1-inch cubes
- 2 tbsp olive oil
- 8 oz mushrooms, halved
- 1/2 tsp garlic powder
- 1 tsp Worcestershire sauce
- Pepper
- Salt

Directions:

1. Add steak cubes and remaining ingredients into the bowl and toss well.
2. Transfer meat mixture to the crispier tray.
3. Place the drip tray below the bottom of the air fryer.
4. Insert the crispier tray into shelf position 4.
5. Select air fry mode. Set the temperature to 400 F and the timer for 18 minutes. Press start.
6. Stir halfway through.
7. Serve and enjoy.

Nutritional Value (Amount per Serving):

- Calories 300
- Fat 12.8 g
- Carbohydrates 2.4 g
- Sugar 1.3 g
- Protein 42.8 g
- Cholesterol 102 mg

Meatballs

Preparation Time: 10 minutes
Cooking Time: 12 minutes
Serve: 6

Ingredients:

- 2 lbs ground beef
- 2 oz pork rind, crushed
- 2 eggs, lightly beaten
- 3 oz parmesan cheese, shredded
- Pepper
- Salt

Directions:

1. Add all ingredients into the bowl and mix until well combined.
2. Make balls from meat mixture and place to crispier tray.
3. Place the drip tray below the bottom of the air fryer.
4. Insert the crispier tray into shelf position 4.
5. Select air fry mode. Set the temperature to 350 F and the timer for 8 minutes. Press start.
6. Turn meatballs and cook for 4 minutes more.

7. Serve and enjoy.

Nutritional Value (Amount per Serving):

- Calories 401
- Fat 17.3 g
- Carbohydrates 0.6 g
- Sugar 0.1 g
- Protein 58.4 g
- Cholesterol 213 mg

Italian Meatballs

Preparation Time: 10 minutes
Cooking Time: 20 minutes
Serve: 4

Ingredients:

- 1 lb ground beef
- 1 tbsp fresh rosemary, chopped
- 2 tbsp marinara sauce
- 2 garlic cloves, minced
- 1/4 cup parmesan cheese, grated
- 1/2 cup breadcrumbs
- 1 egg, lightly beaten
- 1 tbsp fresh basil, chopped
- 1 tbsp fresh parsley, chopped
- Pepper
- Salt

Directions:

1. Add all ingredients into the bowl and mix until well combined.
2. Make balls from meat mixture and place to crispier tray.
3. Place the drip tray below the bottom of the air fryer.
4. Insert the crispier tray into shelf position 4.
5. Select air fry mode. Set the temperature to 375 F and the timer for 20 minutes. Press start.
6. Turn meatballs halfway through.
7. Serve and enjoy.

Nutritional Value (Amount per Serving):

- Calories 310
- Fat 10.5 g
- Carbohydrates 12.2 g
- Sugar 1.6 g
- Protein 39.7 g
- Cholesterol 146 mg

Ranch Beef Patties

Preparation Time: 10 minutes
Cooking Time: 12 minutes
Serve: 4

Ingredients:

- 1 lb ground beef
- 1/2 tsp onion powder
- 1/2 tsp garlic powder
- 2 tsp dried parsley
- 1/8 tsp dried dill
- 1/2 tsp paprika
- 1/2 tsp dried dill
- Pepper
- Salt

Directions:

1. Add all ingredients into the bowl and mix until well combined.
2. Make patties from meat mixture and place to crispier tray.
3. Place the drip tray below the bottom of the air fryer.
4. Insert the crispier tray into shelf position 4.
5. Select air fry mode. Set the temperature to 350 F and the timer for 12 minutes. Press start.
6. Turn patties halfway through.
7. Serve and enjoy.

Nutritional Value (Amount per Serving):

- Calories 214
- Fat 7.1 g
- Carbohydrates 0.8 g
- Sugar 0.2 g
- Protein 34.6 g
- Cholesterol 101 mg

Meatballs

Preparation Time: 10 minutes
Cooking Time: 12 minutes
Serve: 6
Ingredients:

- 1 lb ground beef
- 1/3 cup parmesan cheese, grated
- 1 egg, lightly beaten
- 1/2 onion, diced
- 1/3 cup breadcrumbs
- 1 tbsp garlic, minced
- Pepper
- Salt

Directions:

1. Add all ingredients into the mixing bowl and mix until well combined.
2. Make balls from meat mixture and place to crispier tray.
3. Place the drip tray below the bottom of the air fryer.
4. Insert the crispier tray into shelf position 4.

5. Select air fry mode. Set the temperature to 350 F and the timer for 12 minutes. Press start.
6. Serve and enjoy.

Nutritional Value (Amount per Serving):

- Calories 197
- Fat 6.9 g
- Carbohydrates 5.9 g
- Sugar 0.8 g
- Protein 26.5 g
- Cholesterol 98 mg

Taco Meatballs

Preparation Time: 10 minutes
Cooking Time: 10 minutes
Serve: 4
Ingredients:

- 1 egg, lightly beaten
- 1 lb ground beef
- 1/4 cup onion, chopped
- 2 tbsp taco seasoning
- 1 tbsp garlic, minced
- 1/2 cup cheddar cheese, shredded
- 1/4 cup cilantro, chopped
- Pepper
- Salt

Directions:

1. Add ground beef and remaining ingredients into the bowl and mix until well combined.
2. Make balls from meat mixture and place to crispier tray.
3. Place the drip tray below the bottom of the air fryer.
4. Insert the crispier tray into shelf position 4.
5. Select air fry mode. Set the temperature to 400 F and the timer for 10 minutes. Press start.
6. Serve and enjoy.

Nutritional Value (Amount per Serving):

- Calories 298
- Fat 13.3 g
- Carbohydrates 2.3 g
- Sugar 0.5 g
- Protein 40 g
- Cholesterol 158 mg

Juicy Pork Chops

Preparation Time: 10 minutes
Cooking Time: 12 minutes

Serve: 2

Ingredients:

- 2 pork chops
- 1/2 tsp onion powder
- 1 tsp ground mustard
- 1 tbsp paprika
- 2 tbsp brown sugar
- 1 tbsp olive oil
- 1/4 tsp garlic powder
- Pepper
- Salt

Directions:

1. Add all dry ingredients into the small bowl and mix well.
2. Brush pork chops with oil and rub with spice mixture.
3. Place pork chops on a crispier tray.
4. Place the drip tray below the bottom of the air fryer.
5. Insert the crispier tray into shelf position 4.
6. Select air fry mode. Set the temperature to 400 F and the timer for 12 minutes. Press start.
7. Turn pork chops halfway through.
8. Serve and enjoy.

Nutritional Value (Amount per Serving):

- Calories 371
- Fat 27.8 g
- Carbohydrates 12.1 g
- Sugar 9.5 g
- Protein 19 g
- Cholesterol 69 mg

Honey Garlic Pork Chops

Preparation Time: 10 minutes
Cooking Time: 12 minutes
Serve: 4

Ingredients:

- 4 pork chops
- 2 tbsp lemon juice
- 1/4 cup honey
- 1 tsp garlic, minced
- 1 tbsp olive oil
- 1 tbsp sweet chili sauce
- Pepper
- Salt

Directions:

1. Season pork chops with pepper and salt and place on a crispier tray.
2. Place the drip tray below the bottom of the air fryer.
3. Insert the crispier tray into shelf position 4.

4. Select air fry mode. Set the temperature to 400 F and the timer for 12 minutes. Press start.
5. Turn pork chops halfway through.
6. Meanwhile, heat oil in a pan over medium heat.
7. Add garlic and sauté for 30 seconds.
8. Add remaining ingredients and stir well and cook for 3 minutes.
9. Place pork chops on serving dish.
10. Pour sauce over pork chops and serve.

Nutritional Value (Amount per Serving):

- Calories 361
- Fat 23.4 g
- Carbohydrates 19.4 g
- Sugar 19.1 g
- Protein 18.1 g
- Cholesterol 69 mg

Tender Pork Loin

Preparation Time: 10 minutes
Cooking Time: 18 minutes
Serve: 8
Ingredients:

- 2 lbs pork loin, cut in half to fit in the air fryer basket
- 1 tsp garlic powder
- 3 tbsp brown sugar
- 1 tsp basil
- 1 tsp salt

Directions:

1. Mix brown sugar, basil, garlic powder, and salt and rub all over pork loin and place to the crispier tray.
2. Place the drip tray below the bottom of the air fryer.
3. Insert the crispier tray into shelf position 4.
4. Select air fry mode. Set the temperature to 400 F and the timer for 8 minutes. Press start.
5. Turn pork loin and cook for 10 minutes more.
6. Slice and serve.

Nutritional Value (Amount per Serving):

- Calories 288
- Fat 15.8 g
- Carbohydrates 3.6 g
- Sugar 3.4 g
- Protein 31 g
- Cholesterol 91 mg

Crispy Pork Bites

Preparation Time: 10 minutes
Cooking Time: 15 minutes
Serve: 4
Ingredients:

- 1 lb pork belly, cut into 3/4-inch cubes
- 1/2 tsp garlic powder
- 1/2 tsp onion powder
- 1 tsp soy sauce
- Pepper
- Salt

Directions:

1. In a bowl, toss pork cubes with onion powder, garlic powder, soy sauce, pepper, and salt.
2. Place pork cubes on a crispier tray.
3. Place the drip tray below the bottom of the air fryer.
4. Insert the crispier tray into shelf position 4.
5. Select air fry mode. Set the temperature to 400 F and the timer for 15 minutes. Press start.
6. Turn pork cubes halfway through.
7. Slice and serve.

Nutritional Value (Amount per Serving):

- Calories 526
- Fat 30.5 g
- Carbohydrates 0.6 g
- Sugar 0.2 g
- Protein 52.5 g
- Cholesterol 131 mg

Mustard Honey Pork Chops

Preparation Time: 10 minutes
Cooking Time: 12 minutes
Serve: 4
Ingredients:

- 1 lb pork chops, boneless
- 2 tsp honey
- 1 tbsp yellow mustard
- 1 tsp steak seasoning blend

Directions:

1. In a small bowl, mix honey, mustard, and steak seasoning.
2. Brush pork chops with honey mixture and place on a crispier tray.
3. Place the drip tray below the bottom of the air fryer.

4. Insert the crispier tray into shelf position 4.
5. Select air fry mode. Set the temperature to 350 F and the timer for 12 minutes. Press start.
6. Turn pork chops halfway through.
7. Serve and enjoy.

Nutritional Value (Amount per Serving):

- Calories 376
- Fat 28.3 g
- Carbohydrates 3.1 g
- Sugar 2.9 g
- Protein 25.7 g
- Cholesterol 98 mg

Herb Pork Chops

Preparation Time: 10 minutes
Cooking Time: 15 minutes
Serve: 4
Ingredients:

- 4 pork chops
- 2 tsp oregano
- 2 tsp thyme
- 2 tsp sage
- 1 tsp garlic powder
- 1 tsp paprika
- 1 tsp rosemary
- Pepper
- Salt

Directions:

1. Spray pork chops with cooking spray.
2. Mix garlic powder, paprika, rosemary, oregano, thyme, sage, pepper, and salt and rub over pork chops.
3. Place pork chops on a crispier tray.
4. Place the drip tray below the bottom of the air fryer.
5. Insert the crispier tray into shelf position 4.
6. Select air fry mode. Set the temperature to 360 F and the timer for 15 minutes. Press start.
7. Turn pork chops halfway through.
8. Serve and enjoy.

Nutritional Value (Amount per Serving):

- Calories 266
- Fat 20.2 g
- Carbohydrates 2 g
- Sugar 0.3 g
- Protein 18.4 g
- Cholesterol 69 mg

Meatballs

Preparation Time: 10 minutes
Cooking Time: 10 minutes
Serve: 4
Ingredients:

- 1 1/4 lbs ground pork
- 1 small onion, chopped
- 1 tsp pork seasoning
- 1 tsp garlic paste
- 2 tsp honey
- Pepper
- Salt

Directions:

1. Add all ingredients into the bowl and mix until well combined.
2. Male balls from meat mixture and place to the crispier tray.
3. Place the drip tray below the bottom of the air fryer.
4. Insert the crispier tray into shelf position 4.
5. Select air fry mode. Set the temperature to 350 F and the timer for 10 minutes. Press start.
6. Serve and enjoy.

Nutritional Value (Amount per Serving):

- Calories 221
- Fat 5 g
- Carbohydrates 4.8 g
- Sugar 3.6 g
- Protein 37.3 g
- Cholesterol 103 mg

Meatballs

Preparation Time: 10 minutes
Cooking Time: 20 minutes
Serve: 4
Ingredients:

- 1 egg, lightly beaten
- 1 lb ground lamb
- 2 tsp fresh oregano, chopped
- 2 tbsp fresh parsley, chopped
- 1 tbsp garlic, minced
- 3 tbsp olive oil
- 1/4 tsp red pepper flakes
- 1 tsp ground cumin
- 1/4 tsp pepper
- 1 tsp kosher salt

Directions:

1. Line baking sheet with parchment paper.

2. Add all ingredients except oil into the mixing bowl and mix until well combined.
3. Make balls from the meat mixture and place them on a prepared baking sheet.
4. Drizzle oil over meatballs.
5. Select bake mode. Set the temperature to 425 F and the timer for 20 minutes. Press start.
6. Let the air fryer preheat then insert the pizza rack into shelf position 5.
7. Place baking sheet on the pizza rack and cook.
8. Serve and enjoy.

Nutritional Value (Amount per Serving):

- Calories 325
- Fat 20.2 g
- Carbohydrates 1.7 g
- Sugar 0.2 g
- Protein 33.6 g
- Cholesterol 143 mg

Flavorful Lamb Patties

Preparation Time: 10 minutes
Cooking Time: 15 minutes
Serve: 4
Ingredients:

- 1 lb ground lamb
- 1 tsp ground cumin
- 1 tbsp garlic, minced
- 1/4 tsp cayenne pepper
- 1/2 tsp ground allspice
- 1 tsp ground cinnamon
- 1/4 cup fresh parsley, chopped
- 1/4 cup onion, minced
- 1 tsp ground coriander
- 1/4 tsp pepper
- 1 tsp kosher salt

Directions:

1. Add all ingredients into the large bowl and mix until well combined.
2. Make patties from the meat mixture and place them on a baking sheet.
3. Select bake mode. Set the temperature to 450 F and the timer for 15 minutes. Press start.
4. Let the air fryer preheat then insert the pizza rack into shelf position 5.
5. Place baking sheet on the pizza rack and cook.
6. Serve and enjoy.

Nutritional Value (Amount per Serving):

- Calories 223
- Fat 8.5 g
- Carbohydrates 2.6 g
- Sugar 0.4 g

- Protein 32.3 g
- Cholesterol 102 mg

Chapter 5: Fish & Seafood

Shrimp Scampi

Preparation Time: 10 minutes
Cooking Time: 1 hour 30 minutes
Serve: 4
Ingredients:

- 1 lb raw shrimp, peeled and deveined
- 2 tbsp butter
- 2 tbsp olive oil
- 1/2 cup white cooking wine
- 1/4 cup chicken broth
- 1 tbsp fresh lemon juice
- 2 tbsp fresh parsley, chopped
- 1 tbsp garlic, minced
- Pepper
- Salt

Directions:

1. Add broth, lemon juice, parsley, garlic, butter, olive oil, wine, pepper, and salt into the dutch oven.
2. Add shrimp and stir well and cover the dutch oven with a lid.
3. Insert the pizza rack into shelf position 6.
4. Place dutch oven on pizza rack.
5. Select a slow cook mode. Set the temperature to 225 F and the timer for 1 hour 30 minutes. Press start.
6. Stir well and serve.

Nutritional Value (Amount per Serving):

- Calories 255
- Fat 14.8 g
- Carbohydrates 3.1 g
- Sugar 0.2 g
- Protein 26.4 g
- Cholesterol 254 mg

Herb Salmon

Preparation Time: 10 minutes
Cooking Time: 5 minutes
Serve: 2
Ingredients:

- 2 salmon fillets
- 1 tsp herb de Provence
- 1 tbsp butter, melted
- 2 tbsp olive oil
- Pepper
- Salt

Directions:

1. Brush salmon fillets with oil and sprinkle with herb de Provence, pepper, and salt.
2. Place salmon fillets in crispier tray.
3. Place the drip tray below the bottom of the air fryer.
4. Insert the crispier tray into shelf position 4.
5. Select air fry mode. Set the temperature to 390 F and the timer for 5 minutes. Press start.
6. Drizzle butter over salmon and serve.

Nutritional Value (Amount per Serving):

- Calories 410
- Fat 31 g
- Carbohydrates 0 g
- Sugar 0 g
- Protein 35.1 g
- Cholesterol 94 mg

Salmon Cakes

Preparation Time: 10 minutes
Cooking Time: 7 minutes
Serve: 2

Ingredients:

- 8 oz salmon fillet, minced
- 1 egg, lightly beaten
- 1/4 tsp garlic powder
- Pepper
- Salt

Directions:

1. Add all ingredients into the bowl and mix until just combined.
2. Make small patties from the salmon mixture and place them in a crispier tray.
3. Place the drip tray below the bottom of the air fryer.
4. Insert the crispier tray into shelf position 4.
5. Select air fry mode. Set the temperature to 390 F and the timer for 7 minutes. Press start.
6. Serve and enjoy.

Nutritional Value (Amount per Serving):

- Calories 183
- Fat 9.2 g
- Carbohydrates 0.5 g
- Sugar 0.3 g
- Protein 24.8 g
- Cholesterol 132 mg

Salmon with Carrots

Preparation Time: 10 minutes
Cooking Time: 20 minutes
Serve: 4
Ingredients:

- 1 lb salmon, cut into four pieces
- 2 cups baby carrots
- 2 tbsp olive oil
- Salt

Directions:

1. Place salmon pieces on the center of the baking sheet.
2. In a bowl, toss together baby carrots and olive oil.
3. Arrange carrot around the salmon.
4. Select bake mode. Set the temperature to 425 F and the timer for 20 minutes. Press start.
5. Let the air fryer preheat then insert the pizza rack into shelf position 5.
6. Place baking sheet on the pizza rack and cook.
7. Season with salt and serve.

Nutritional Value (Amount per Serving):

- Calories 212
- Fat 14 g
- Carbohydrates 0.4 g
- Sugar 0.2 g
- Protein 22 g
- Cholesterol 50 mg

Rosemary Salmon

Preparation Time: 10 minutes
Cooking Time: 15 minutes
Serve: 4
Ingredients:

- 1 lbs salmon, cut into 4 pieces
- 1/4 tsp dried basil
- 1 tbsp dried chives
- 1 tbsp olive oil
- 1/2 tbsp dried rosemary
- Pepper
- Salt

Directions:

1. Place salmon pieces skin side down in the crisper tray.
2. In a small bowl, mix together olive oil, basil, chives, and rosemary.
3. Brush salmon with oil mixture.

4. Place the drip tray below the bottom of the air fryer.
5. Insert the crispier tray into shelf position 4.
6. Select air fry mode. Set the temperature to 400 F and the timer for 15 minutes. Press start.
7. Serve and enjoy.

Nutritional Value (Amount per Serving):

- Calories 182
- Fat 10.6 g
- Carbohydrates 0.3 g
- Sugar 0 g
- Protein 22 g
- Cholesterol 50 mg

Baked Fish Fillets with Pepper

Preparation Time: 10 minutes
Cooking Time: 30 minutes
Serve: 1

Ingredients:

- 8 oz frozen white fish fillet
- 1 tbsp fresh parsley, chopped
- 1 tbsp roasted red bell pepper, diced
- 1/2 tsp Italian seasoning
- 1 1/2 tbsp butter, melted
- 1 tbsp lemon juice

Directions:

1. Place the fish fillet in a baking dish.
2. Drizzle butter and lemon juice over fish.
3. Sprinkle with Italian seasoning.
4. Top with roasted bell pepper and parsley.
5. Select bake mode. Set the temperature to 400 F and the timer for 30 minutes. Press start.
6. Let the air fryer preheat then insert the pizza rack into shelf position 5.
7. Place baking dish on the pizza rack and cook.
8. Serve and enjoy.

Nutritional Value (Amount per Serving):

- Calories 357
- Fat 18.8 g
- Carbohydrates 1.3 g
- Sugar 0.8 g
- Protein 46.8 g
- Cholesterol 47 mg

Lemon Herb Fish Fillets

Preparation Time: 10 minutes
Cooking Time: 10 minutes
Serve: 4
Ingredients:

- 24 oz salmon, cut into 4 pieces
- 1 garlic clove, grated
- 1 tbsp yogurt
- 1 tsp lemon zest
- 2 tbsp lemon juice
- 2 tbsp olive oil
- 1 tsp oregano
- 1/4 tsp pepper
- 1/4 tsp salt

Directions:

1. Add all ingredients except salmon to a baking dish and mix well.
2. Add salmon and coat well and let it sit for 30 minutes.
3. Select bake mode. Set the temperature to 400 F and the timer for 10 minutes. Press start.
4. Let the air fryer preheat then insert the pizza rack into shelf position 5.
5. Place baking dish on the pizza rack and cook.
6. Serve and enjoy.

Nutritional Value (Amount per Serving):

- Calories 292
- Fat 17.7 g
- Carbohydrates 1.1 g
- Sugar 0.5 g
- Protein 33.4 g
- Cholesterol 75 mg

Greek Salmon

Preparation Time: 10 minutes
Cooking Time: 20 minutes
Serve: 5
Ingredients:

- 1 3/4 lbs salmon fillet
- 1/3 cup basil pesto
- 1 tbsp fresh dill, chopped
- 1/4 cup capers
- 1/3 cup artichoke hearts
- 1/4 cup sun-dried tomatoes, drained
- 1/4 cup olives, pitted and chopped
- 1 tsp paprika
- 1/4 tsp salt

Directions:

1. Line baking sheet with parchment paper.
2. Arrange salmon fillet on a prepared baking sheet and sprinkle with paprika and salt.
3. Add remaining ingredients on top of salmon.
4. Select bake mode. Set the temperature to 400 F and the timer for 20 minutes. Press start.
5. Let the air fryer preheat then insert the pizza rack into shelf position 5.
6. Place baking sheet on the pizza rack and cook.
7. Serve and enjoy.

Nutritional Value (Amount per Serving):

- Calories 228
- Fat 10.7 g
- Carbohydrates 2.6 g
- Sugar 0.4 g
- Protein 31.6 g
- Cholesterol 70 mg

Italian Tilapia

Preparation Time: 10 minutes
Cooking Time: 17 minutes
Serve: 2

Ingredients:

- 1/2 lb tilapia fillets, remove bones
- 2 oz feta cheese, crumbled
- 2/3 cup tomatoes, chopped
- 1 1/2 tbsp garlic, minced
- 1/3 cup fresh parsley, chopped
- 1 tsp olive oil
- Pepper
- Salt

Directions:

1. In a bowl, mix tomatoes, garlic, feta, parsley, and olive oil.
2. Spray tilapia fillets with cooking spray and season with pepper and salt.
3. Place tilapia fillets on a baking sheet and top and with tomato mixture.
4. Select bake mode. Set the temperature to 400 F and the timer for 17 minutes. Press start.
5. Let the air fryer preheat then insert the pizza rack into shelf position 5.
6. Place baking sheet on the pizza rack and cook.
7. Serve and enjoy.

Nutritional Value (Amount per Serving):

- Calories 212
- Fat 9.6 g
- Carbohydrates 6.2 g
- Sugar 2.9 g
- Protein 26.4 g
- Cholesterol 80 mg

Baked Cod

Preparation Time: 10 minutes
Cooking Time: 10 minutes
Serve: 2

Ingredients:

- 1 lb cod fillets
- 1 tbsp fresh parsley, chopped
- 1/8 tsp cayenne pepper
- 1 tbsp fresh lemon juice
- 1 1/2 tbsp olive oil
- 1/4 tsp salt

Directions:

1. Place fish fillets on the baking sheet.
2. Drizzle with oil and lemon juice and season with cayenne pepper and salt.
3. Select bake mode. Set the temperature to 400 F and the timer for 10 minutes. Press start.
4. Let the air fryer preheat then insert the pizza rack into shelf position 5.
5. Place baking sheet on the pizza rack and cook.
6. Garnish with parsley and serve.

Nutritional Value (Amount per Serving):

- Calories 275
- Fat 12.6 g
- Carbohydrates 0.3 g
- Sugar 0.2 g
- Protein 40.6 g
- Cholesterol 111 mg

Baked Lemon Pepper Basa

Preparation Time: 10 minutes
Cooking Time: 12 minutes
Serve: 4

Ingredients:

- 4 basa fish fillets
- 1/4 tsp lemon pepper seasoning
- 4 tbsp fresh lemon juice
- 8 tsp olive oil
- 2 tbsp fresh parsley, chopped
- 1/4 cup green onion, sliced
- 1/2 tsp garlic powder
- Pepper
- Salt

Directions:

1. Place fish fillets in a baking dish.
2. Pour oil and lemon juice over fish fillets. Sprinkle remaining ingredients.

3. Select bake mode. Set the temperature to 425 F and the timer for 12 minutes. Press start.
4. Let the air fryer preheat then insert the pizza rack into shelf position 5.
5. Place baking dish on the pizza rack and cook.
6. Serve and enjoy.

Nutritional Value (Amount per Serving):

- Calories 308
- Fat 21.4 g
- Carbohydrates 5.5 g
- Sugar 3.4 g
- Protein 24.1 g
- Cholesterol 0 mg

Cajun Fish Fillets

Preparation Time: 10 minutes
Cooking Time: 15 minutes
Serve: 4

Ingredients:

- 1 lb catfish fillets, cut 1/2-inch thick
- 1/2 tsp ground cumin
- 3/4 tsp chili powder
- 1 tsp crushed red pepper
- 2 tsp onion powder
- 1 tbsp dried oregano, crushed
- Pepper
- Salt

Directions:

1. In a small bowl, mix cumin, chili powder, crushed red pepper, onion powder, oregano, pepper, and salt.
2. Rub fish fillets with the spice mixture and place in a baking dish.
3. Select bake mode. Set the temperature to 350 F and the timer for 15 minutes. Press start.
4. Let the air fryer preheat then insert the pizza rack into shelf position 5.
5. Place baking dish on the pizza rack and cook.
6. Serve and enjoy.

Nutritional Value (Amount per Serving):

- Calories 165
- Fat 9 g
- Carbohydrates 2.4 g
- Sugar 0.6 g
- Protein 18 g
- Cholesterol 53 mg

Garlic Halibut

Preparation Time: 10 minutes
Cooking Time: 12 minutes
Serve: 4
Ingredients:

- 1 lb halibut fillets
- 1/4 tsp garlic powder
- 1/2 tsp paprika
- 1/4 cup olive oil
- Pepper
- Salt

Directions:

1. Place fish fillets in a baking dish.
2. In a small bowl, mix together oil, garlic powder, paprika, pepper, and salt.
3. Brush fish fillets with oil mixture.
4. Select bake mode. Set the temperature to 425 F and the timer for 12 minutes. Press start.
5. Let the air fryer preheat then insert the pizza rack into shelf position 5.
6. Place baking dish on the pizza rack and cook.
7. Serve and enjoy.

Nutritional Value (Amount per Serving):

- Calories 235
- Fat 15.3 g
- Carbohydrates 0.3 g
- Sugar 0.1 g
- Protein 23.9 g
- Cholesterol 36 mg

Parmesan Shrimp

Preparation Time: 10 minutes
Cooking Time: 10 minutes
Serve: 3
Ingredients:

- 1 lb shrimp, peeled and deveined
- 1 tbsp olive oil
- 1/4 tsp oregano
- 1/2 tsp pepper
- 1/4 cup parmesan cheese, grated
- 3 garlic cloves, minced
- 1/2 tsp onion powder
- 1/2 tsp basil

Directions:

1. Add all ingredients into the large bowl and toss well.
2. Add shrimp into the crisper tray.

3. Place the drip tray below the bottom of the air fryer.
4. Insert the crispier tray into shelf position 4.
5. Select air fry mode. Set the temperature to 350 F and the timer for 10 minutes. Press start.
6. Serve and enjoy.

Nutritional Value (Amount per Serving):

- Calories 251
- Fat 8.9 g
- Carbohydrates 4.2 g
- Sugar 0.2 g
- Protein 37.1 g
- Cholesterol 324 mg

Delicious Tuna Cakes

Preparation Time: 10 minutes
Cooking Time: 6 minutes
Serve: 4
Ingredients:

- 1 egg, lightly beaten
- 8 oz can tuna, drained
- 1 tbsp mustard
- 1/4 cup almond flour
- Pepper
- Salt

Directions:

1. Add all ingredients into the large bowl and mix until just combined.
2. Make patties from the mixture and place them in the crisper tray.
3. Place the drip tray below the bottom of the air fryer.
4. Insert the crispier tray into shelf position 4.
5. Select air fry mode. Set the temperature to 400 F and the timer for 6 minutes. Press start.
6. Turn patties halfway through.
7. Serve and enjoy.

Nutritional Value (Amount per Serving):

- Calories 137
- Fat 5.7 g
- Carbohydrates 2.6 g
- Sugar 0.3 g
- Protein 18 g
- Cholesterol 58 mg

Blackened Shrimp

Preparation Time: 10 minutes
Cooking Time: 6 minutes

Serve: 4

Ingredients:

- 1 lb shrimp, peeled and deveined
- 2 tbsp olive oil
- 2 tsp paprika
- 1/4 tsp cayenne
- 1 tsp dried oregano
- 1 tsp garlic powder
- 1 tsp onion powder
- Pepper
- Salt

Directions:

1. In a large bowl, toss shrimp with remaining ingredients.
2. Transfer shrimp to the crispier tray.
3. Place the drip tray below the bottom of the air fryer.
4. Insert the crispier tray into shelf position 4.
5. Select air fry mode. Set the temperature to 400 F and the timer for 6 minutes. Press start.
6. Serve and enjoy.

Nutritional Value (Amount per Serving):

- Calories 204
- Fat 9.1 g
- Carbohydrates 3.6 g
- Sugar 0.5 g
- Protein 26.2 g
- Cholesterol 239 mg

Cajun Salmon

Preparation Time: 10 minutes
Cooking Time: 12 minutes
Serve: 4

Ingredients:

- 4 salmon fillets
- 4 tbsp brown sugar
- 2 tsp Cajun seasoning
- Salt

Directions:

1. Line baking sheet with foil and set aside.
2. Mix together Cajun seasoning, brown sugar, and salt and rub all over salmon.
3. Place salmon on a baking sheet.
4. Select bake mode. Set the temperature to 390 F and the timer for 12 minutes. Press start.
5. Let the air fryer preheat then insert the pizza rack into shelf position 5.
6. Place baking sheet on the pizza rack and cook.
7. Serve and enjoy.

Nutritional Value (Amount per Serving):

- Calories 270
- Fat 11 g
- Carbohydrates 8.8 g
- Sugar 8.7 g
- Protein 34.6 g
- Cholesterol 78 mg

Dijon Salmon

Preparation Time: 10 minutes
Cooking Time: 12 minutes
Serve: 4
Ingredients:

- 4 salmon fillets
- 3 tbsp maple syrup
- 2 tbsp ground Dijon mustard

Directions:

1. Line baking sheet with parchment paper and set aside.
2. Arrange salmon fillets on a baking sheet.
3. Mix together Dijon mustard and maple syrup and brush over salmon fillets.
4. Select bake mode. Set the temperature to 390 F and the timer for 12 minutes. Press start.
5. Let the air fryer preheat then insert the pizza rack into shelf position 5.
6. Place baking sheet on the pizza rack and cook.
7. Serve and enjoy.

Nutritional Value (Amount per Serving):

- Calories 282
- Fat 11 g
- Carbohydrates 10.1 g
- Sugar 8.9 g
- Protein 34.5 g
- Cholesterol 78 mg

Scallop Gratin

Preparation Time: 10 minutes
Cooking Time: 8 minutes
Serve: 4
Ingredients:

- 1 1/2 lbs sea scallops
- 1/4 cup white wine
- 1/4 cup cream cheese, softened
- 1/4 cup parmesan cheese, shaved
- 1 tbsp tarragon, chopped
- 1 lemon juice
- Pepper
- Salt

Directions:

1. Add scallops to the baking dish.
2. In a bowl, whisk lemon juice, cream cheese, white wine, tarragon, parmesan cheese, pepper, and salt and pour over scallops.
3. Select bake mode. Set the temperature to 390 F and the timer for 8 minutes. Press start.
4. Let the air fryer preheat then insert the pizza rack into shelf position 5.
5. Place baking dish on the pizza rack and cook.
6. Serve and enjoy.

Nutritional Value (Amount per Serving):

- Calories 235
- Fat 7.7 g
- Carbohydrates 5.5 g
- Sugar 0.4 g
- Protein 31.6 g
- Cholesterol 76 mg

Baked Crab Patties

Preparation Time: 10 minutes
Cooking Time: 30 minutes
Serve: 6

Ingredients:

- 16 oz lump crab meat
- 1 cup crushed crackers
- 1 tsp old bay seasoning
- 1 tsp brown mustard
- 2/3 cup mashed avocado
- 1/4 cup celery, diced
- 1/4 cup onion, diced

Directions:

1. Line baking sheet with parchment paper and set aside.
2. Add all ingredients into the mixing bowl and mix until well combined.
3. Make patties from the mixture and place them on a baking sheet.
4. Select bake mode. Set the temperature to 350 F and the timer for 30 minutes. Press start.
5. Let the air fryer preheat then insert the pizza rack into shelf position 5.
6. Place baking sheet on the pizza rack and cook.
7. Serve and enjoy.

Nutritional Value (Amount per Serving):

- Calories 84
- Fat 7.7 g
- Carbohydrates 4.6 g
- Sugar 0.8 g
- Protein 11.5 g
- Cholesterol 43 mg

Chapter 6: Vegetables & Side Dishes

Flavorful Potato Casserole

Preparation Time: 10 minute
Cooking Time: 30 minutes
Serve: 6
Ingredients:

- 2 lb potatoes, peel & shredded
- 1 1/2 cups sour cream
- 2 cups cheddar cheese, shredded
- 1/4 cup parsley, chopped
- 1/4 cup dill, chopped
- 1 small onion, minced
- Pepper
- Salt

Directions:

1. Spray a 9-inch baking pan with cooking spray and set aside.
2. Add all ingredients into the mixing bowl and mix until well combined.
3. Pour mixture into the prepared baking pan.
4. Select bake mode. Set the temperature to 425 F and the timer for 30 minutes. Press start.
5. Let the air fryer preheat then insert the pizza rack into shelf position 5.
6. Place baking pan on the pizza rack and bake.
7. Serve and enjoy.

Nutritional Value (Amount per Serving):

- Calories 328
- Fat 24.7 g
- Carbohydrates 15.5 g
- Sugar 1.2 g
- Protein 13 g
- Cholesterol 65 mg

Butternut Squash Cubes

Preparation Time: 10 minutes
Cooking Time: 30 minutes
Serve: 6
Ingredients:

- 2 lbs butternut squash, peel & cut into 1/2-inch cubes
- 2 tsp thyme, chopped
- 2 garlic cloves, crushed
- 2 tbsp maple syrup
- 2 tbsp olive oil
- 1 tsp salt

Directions:

1. In a small bowl, whisk oil, thyme, garlic, maple syrup, and salt.
2. Add butternut squash into the mixing bowl. Pour oil mixture over butternut squash and toss well.
3. Spread butternut squash on a baking sheet.
4. Select bake mode. Set the temperature to 400 F and the timer for 30 minutes. Press start.
5. Let the air fryer preheat then insert the pizza rack into shelf position 5.
6. Place baking sheet on the pizza rack and bake.
7. Serve and enjoy.

Nutritional Value (Amount per Serving):
- Calories 128
- Fat 4.9 g
- Carbohydrates 22.7 g
- Sugar 7.3 g
- Protein 1.6 g
- Cholesterol 0 mg

Cheesy Baked Cabbage

Preparation Time: 10 minutes
Cooking Time: 10 minutes
Serve: 6

Ingredients:
- 2 medium cabbage heads, cored & cut into 2-inch pieces
- 2 tbsp white sugar
- 3 tbsp flour
- 4 tbsp butter, melted
- 1 1/2 cups milk
- 1/2 tbsp white pepper
- 3/4 cup Swiss cheese, shredded
- 3/4 cup American cheese, shredded
- 1 tbsp salt

Directions:
1. Steam the cabbage. In a mixing bowl, mix cabbage, sugar, flour, butter, milk, and salt.
2. Transfer cabbage mixture into the baking dish. Sprinkle cheese on top.
3. Select bake mode. Set the temperature to 350 F and the timer for 10 minutes. Press start.
4. Let the air fryer preheat then insert the pizza rack into shelf position 5.
5. Place baking dish on the pizza rack and bake.
6. Serve and enjoy.

Nutritional Value (Amount per Serving):
- Calories 303
- Fat 16.6 g

- Carbohydrates 29.7 g
- Sugar 17.7 g
- Protein 12.7 g
- Cholesterol 49 mg

Perfect Cheese Broccoli Bake

Preparation Time: 10 minutes
Cooking Time: 35 minutes
Serve: 10
Ingredients:
- 1 lb broccoli florets
- 2 eggs, lightly beaten
- 1 3/4 cups Swiss cheese, shredded
- 2 cups of milk
- 3 tbsp flour
- 3 1/2 tbsp butter
- 1 1/2 tsp salt

Directions:
1. Spray 10*7-inch baking dish with cooking spray and set aside.
2. Add broccoli to boiling water and cook for 10 minutes. Drain well.
3. Melt butter in a pot over low heat. Add flour and salt and whisk until smooth.
4. Slowly add milk and whisk constantly until thickened, about 2 minutes. Remove pot from heat.
5. Add broccoli and cheese and stir to combine. Add eggs and stit to combine.
6. Pour the broccoli mixture into the prepared baking dish.
7. Select bake mode. Set the temperature to 325 F and the timer for 35 minutes. Press start.
8. Let the air fryer preheat then insert the pizza rack into shelf position 5.
9. Place baking dish on the pizza rack and bake.
10. Serve and enjoy.

Nutritional Value (Amount per Serving):
- Calories 168
- Fat 11.3 g
- Carbohydrates 8.3 g
- Sugar 3.3 g
- Protein 9.4 g
- Cholesterol 65 mg

Spinach Zucchini Casserole

Preparation Time: 10 minutes
Cooking Time: 40 minutes
Serve: 6
Ingredients:

- 2 egg whites
- 2 tsp garlic powder
- 1/2 tsp pepper
- 1/4 cup parmesan cheese, grated
- 2 small yellow squash, diced
- 1/2 cup breadcrumbs
- 1 tsp dried basil
- 2 small zucchini, diced
- 1/4 cup feta cheese, crumbled
- 3 cups baby spinach
- 1 tbsp olive oil
- 1/2 tsp kosher salt

Directions:

1. Spray 9*13-inch casserole dish with cooking spray and set aside.
2. Heat oil in a pan over medium heat.
3. Add zucchini, yellow squash, and spinach and cook until spinach is wilted about 5 minutes.
4. Transfer zucchini mixture into the mixing bowl. Add remaining ingredients and mix well.
5. Spread mixture into the prepared casserole dish.
6. Select bake mode. Set the temperature to 400 F and the timer for 40 minutes. Press start.
7. Let the air fryer preheat then insert the pizza rack into shelf position 5.
8. Place casserole dish on the pizza rack and bake.
9. Serve and enjoy.

Nutritional Value (Amount per Serving):

- Calories 109
- Fat 5.2 g
- Carbohydrates 10.9 g
- Sugar 2.6 g
- Protein 6.1 g
- Cholesterol 8 mg

Tomato Squash Zucchini Bake

Preparation Time: 10 minutes
Cooking Time: 30 minutes
Serve: 6
Ingredients:

- 3 tomatoes, sliced
- 2 medium zucchinis, sliced
- 3/4 cup parmesan cheese, shredded
- 1 tbsp olive oil
- 2 yellow squash, sliced
- Pepper
- Salt

Directions:

1. Spray a 9*13-inch baking dish with cooking spray and set aside.

2. Arrange sliced tomatoes, squash, and zucchinis alternately in the baking dish.
3. Drizzle with oil and season with pepper and salt.
4. Sprinkle parmesan cheese on top of vegetables.
5. Select bake mode. Set the temperature to 350 F and the timer for 30 minutes. Press start.
6. Let the air fryer preheat then insert the pizza rack into shelf position 5.
7. Place baking dish on the pizza rack and cook.
8. Serve and enjoy.

Nutritional Value (Amount per Serving):

- Calories 88
- Fat 5.1 g
- Carbohydrates 7.2 g
- Sugar 3.9 g
- Protein 5.7 g
- Cholesterol 8 mg

Baked Vegetables

Preparation Time: 10 minutes
Cooking Time: 35 minutes
Serve: 4
Ingredients:

- 3 cups Brussels sprouts, cut in half
- 2 zucchini, cut into 1/2-inch thick half circles
- 2 bell peppers, cut into 2-inch chunks
- 1 tsp thyme
- 8 oz mushrooms, cut in half
- 1 onion, cut into wedges
- 2 tbsp vinegar
- 1/4 cup olive oil
- 1/2 tsp salt

Directions:

1. Line baking sheet with parchment paper and set aside.
2. Add vegetables into the zip-lock bag.
3. Mix thyme, vinegar, oil, and salt and pour over vegetables.
4. Seal zip-lock bag and shake well and place it in the refrigerator for 1 hour.
5. Spread marinated vegetables on a baking sheet.
6. Select bake mode. Set the temperature to 375 F and the timer for 35 minutes. Press start.
7. Let the air fryer preheat then insert the pizza rack into shelf position 5.
8. Place baking sheet on the pizza rack and cook.
9. Serve and enjoy.

Nutritional Value (Amount per Serving):

- Calories 197
- Fat 13.4 g
- Carbohydrates 18.4 g
- Sugar 8.3 g
- Protein 6.1 g
- Cholesterol 0 mg

Cheesy Brussels Sprouts

Preparation Time: 10 minutes
Cooking Time: 25 minutes
Serve: 4
Ingredients:

- 15 oz Brussels sprouts, trimmed and cut in half
- 1/4 cup parmesan cheese, grated
- 3 garlic cloves, minced
- 1/4 cup breadcrumbs
- 3 tbsp olive oil
- Pepper
- Salt

Directions:
1. Line baking sheet with parchment paper and set aside.
2. In a bowl, toss Brussels sprouts with breadcrumbs, cheese, garlic, oil, pepper, and salt until well coated.
3. Arrange Brussels sprouts on a baking sheet.
4. Select bake mode. Set the temperature to 390 F and the timer for 25 minutes. Press start.
5. Let the air fryer preheat then insert the pizza rack into shelf position 5.
6. Place baking sheet on the pizza rack and cook.
7. Serve and enjoy.

Nutritional Value (Amount per Serving):
- Calories 184
- Fat 12.4 g
- Carbohydrates 15.5 g
- Sugar 2.7 g
- Protein 6.5 g
- Cholesterol 4 mg

Healthy Zucchini Bake

Preparation Time: 10 minutes
Cooking Time: 45 minutes
Serve: 6
Ingredients:

- 3 zucchini, grated
- 1/2 cup mozzarella cheese, shredded

- 1/2 cup feta cheese, crumbled
- 1/2 cup dill, chopped
- 3 eggs, lightly beaten
- 3 tbsp butter, melted
- 1/2 cup flour
- Pepper
- Salt

Directions:
1. Spray a 9-inch baking dish with cooking spray and set aside.
2. In a bowl, mix together zucchini, cheeses, dill, eggs, butter, pepper, flour, and salt.
3. Pour the zucchini mixture into the baking dish.
4. Select bake mode. Set the temperature to 350 F and the timer for 45 minutes. Press start.
5. Let the air fryer preheat then insert the pizza rack into shelf position 5.
6. Place baking dish on the pizza rack and cook.
7. Serve and enjoy.

Nutritional Value (Amount per Serving):
- Calories 186
- Fat 11.5 g
- Carbohydrates 14.2 g
- Sugar 2.4 g
- Protein 8.4 g
- Cholesterol 109 mg

Green Bean Casserole

Preparation Time: 10 minutes
Cooking Time: 25 minutes
Serve: 4

Ingredients:
- 1 lb green beans, trimmed and cut into pieces
- 1/4 cup parmesan cheese, shredded
- 1/4 cup olive oil
- 2 oz pecans, crushed
- 1 small onion, chopped
- 2 tbsp lemon zest

Directions:
1. Add all ingredients into the bowl and toss well.
2. Spread green bean mixture into the baking dish.
3. Select bake mode. Set the temperature to 390 F and the timer for 25 minutes. Press start.
4. Let the air fryer preheat then insert the pizza rack into shelf position 5.
5. Place baking dish on the pizza rack and cook.
6. Serve and enjoy.

Nutritional Value (Amount per Serving):

- Calories 269
- Fat 24.1 g
- Carbohydrates 12.6 g
- Sugar 3 g
- Protein 5.7 g
- Cholesterol 4 mg

Eggplant Zucchini Casserole

Preparation Time: 10 minutes
Cooking Time: 35 minutes
Serve: 6
Ingredients:

- 3 zucchini, sliced
- 4 tbsp basil, chopped
- 3 oz parmesan cheese, grated
- 1/4 cup parsley, chopped
- 1 cup cherry tomatoes, halved
- 1 medium eggplant, sliced
- 1 tbsp olive oil
- 3 garlic cloves, minced
- 1/4 tsp pepper
- 1/4 tsp salt

Directions:

1. Spray a baking dish with cooking spray and set aside.
2. Add all ingredients into the large bowl and toss well to combine.
3. Pour eggplant mixture into the baking dish.
4. Select bake mode. Set the temperature to 350 F and the timer for 35 minutes. Press start.
5. Let the air fryer preheat then insert the pizza rack into shelf position 5.
6. Place baking dish on the pizza rack and cook.
7. Serve and enjoy.

Nutritional Value (Amount per Serving):

- Calories 109
- Fat 5.8 g
- Carbohydrates 10.2 g
- Sugar 4.8 g
- Protein 7 g
- Cholesterol 10 mg

Air Fryer Brussels Sprouts

Preparation Time: 10 minutes
Cooking Time: 14 minutes
Serve: 2
Ingredients:

- 1/2 lb Brussels sprouts, trimmed and halved
- 1/2 tsp chili powder
- 1/2 tbsp olive oil

- 1 tbsp chives, chopped
- 1/4 tsp cayenne
- Pepper
- Salt

Directions:

1. Add all ingredients into the large bowl and toss well.
2. Spread Brussels sprouts in a crispier tray.
3. Place the drip tray below the bottom of the air fryer.
4. Insert the crispier tray into shelf position 4.
5. Select air fry mode. Set the temperature to 370 F and the timer for 14 minutes. Press start.
6. Serve and enjoy.

Nutritional Value (Amount per Serving):

- Calories 82
- Fat 4.1 g
- Carbohydrates 10.9 g
- Sugar 2.6 g
- Protein 4 g
- Cholesterol 0 mg

Rosemary Garlic Potatoes

Preparation Time: 10 minutes
Cooking Time: 15 minutes
Serve: 4

Ingredients:

- 4 cups baby potatoes, cut into four pieces each
- 2 tsp dried rosemary, minced
- 3 tbsp olive oil
- 1/4 cup fresh parsley, chopped
- 1 tbsp garlic, minced
- 1 tbsp fresh lemon juice
- Pepper
- Salt

Directions:

1. In a large bowl, add potatoes, garlic, rosemary, oil, pepper, and salt and toss well.
2. Spread potatoes in a crispier tray.
3. Place the drip tray below the bottom of the air fryer.
4. Insert the crispier tray into shelf position 4.
5. Select air fry mode. Set the temperature to 400 F and the timer for 15 minutes. Press start.
6. Transfer roasted potatoes in a bowl and toss with parsley and lemon juice.
7. Serve and enjoy.

Nutritional Value (Amount per Serving):

- Calories 148
- Fat 10.8 g

- Carbohydrates 12.3 g
- Sugar 0.1 g
- Protein 2.6 g
- Cholesterol 0 mg

Stuffed Peppers

Preparation Time: 10 minutes
Cooking Time: 25 minutes
Serve: 6
Ingredients:

- 3 bell peppers, cut in half & remove seeds
- 1/4 cup feta cheese, crumbled
- 1/2 cup grape tomatoes, sliced
- 1/3 cup chickpeas, rinsed
- 1/2 tsp oregano
- 2 garlic cloves, minced
- 1 1/2 cups cooked quinoa
- 1/2 tsp salt

Directions:

1. In a bowl, mix cooked quinoa, tomatoes, chickpeas, oregano, garlic, and salt.
2. Stuff quinoa mixture into the bell pepper halves and place in a baking dish.
3. Select bake mode. Set the temperature to 400 F and the timer for 25 minutes. Press start.
4. Let the air fryer preheat then insert the pizza rack into shelf position 5.
5. Place baking dish on the pizza rack and cook.
6. Top peppers with crumbled cheese and serve.

Nutritional Value (Amount per Serving):

- Calories 237
- Fat 4.8 g
- Carbohydrates 39.8 g
- Sugar 4.9 g
- Protein 9.8 g
- Cholesterol 6 mg

Air Fryer Garlic Mushrooms

Preparation Time: 10 minutes
Cooking Time: 15 minutes
Serve: 4
Ingredients:

- 15 oz baby portobello mushrooms, halved
- 2 tbsp butter, melted
- 2 tsp coconut aminos
- 2 tsp garlic, minced

Directions:

1. In a bowl, toss mushrooms with coconut aminos, garlic, and butter.
2. Add mushrooms to the crispier tray.
3. Place the drip tray below the bottom of the air fryer.
4. Insert the crispier tray into shelf position 4.
5. Select air fry mode. Set the temperature to 400 F and the timer for 15 minutes. Press start.
6. Serve and enjoy.

Nutritional Value (Amount per Serving):
- Calories 321
- Fat 5.8 g
- Carbohydrates 40.8 g
- Sugar 0 g
- Protein 40 g
- Cholesterol 15 mg

Lemon Cheese Asparagus

Preparation Time: 10 minutes
Cooking Time: 10 minutes
Serve: 4
Ingredients:
- 1 lb asparagus, cut woody ends and trimmed
- 1 tbsp fresh lemon juice
- 1 tsp olive oil
- 1 oz feta cheese, crumbled
- Pepper
- Salt

Directions:
1. Toss asparagus with lemon juice, olive oil, pepper, and salt in a bowl.
2. Add asparagus to a crispier tray.
3. Place the drip tray below the bottom of the air fryer.
4. Insert the crispier tray into shelf position 4.
5. Select air fry mode. Set the temperature to 400 F and the timer for 10 minutes. Press start.
6. Top with feta cheese and serve.

Nutritional Value (Amount per Serving):
- Calories 52
- Fat 2.9 g
- Carbohydrates 4.8 g
- Sugar 2.5 g
- Protein 3.5 g
- Cholesterol 6 mg

Tasty Green Beans with Onion

Preparation Time: 10 minutes
Cooking Time: 6 minutes
Serve: 4
Ingredients:

- 1 lb green beans, trimmed
- 1/2 cup onion, sliced
- 2 tbsp olive oil
- Pepper
- Salt

Directions:

1. In a bowl, toss green beans with oil, sliced onion, pepper, and salt.
2. Add green beans and onion to the crispier tray.
3. Place the drip tray below the bottom of the air fryer.
4. Insert the crispier tray into shelf position 4.
5. Select air fry mode. Set the temperature to 330 F and the timer for 6 minutes. Press start.
6. Serve and enjoy.

Nutritional Value (Amount per Serving):

- Calories 101
- Fat 7.2 g
- Carbohydrates 9.5 g
- Sugar 2.2 g
- Protein 2.2 g
- Cholesterol 0 mg

Curried Cauliflower Florets

Preparation Time: 10 minutes
Cooking Time: 10 minutes
Serve: 4
Ingredients:

- 1 small cauliflower head, cut into florets
- 1 tbsp curry powder
- 2 tbsp olive oil
- 1/4 tsp salt

Directions:

1. In a bowl, toss cauliflower florets with oil, curry powder, and salt.
2. Add cauliflower florets in a crispier tray.
3. Place the drip tray below the bottom of the air fryer.
4. Insert the crispier tray into shelf position 4.

5. Select air fry mode. Set the temperature to 350 F and the timer for 10 minutes. Press start.
6. Serve and enjoy.

Nutritional Value (Amount per Serving):

- Calories 82
- Fat 7.3 g
- Carbohydrates 4.4 g
- Sugar 1.6 g
- Protein 1.5 g
- Cholesterol 0 mg

Flavorful Cauliflower Florets

Preparation Time: 10 minutes
Cooking Time: 20 minutes
Serve: 4
Ingredients:

- 5 cups cauliflower florets
- 6 garlic cloves, chopped
- 4 tablespoons olive oil
- 1/2 tsp cumin powder
- 1/2 tsp ground coriander
- 1/2 tsp salt

Directions:

1. Add cauliflower florets and remaining ingredients into the large bowl and toss well.
2. Add cauliflower florets in a crispier tray.
3. Place the drip tray below the bottom of the air fryer.
4. Insert the crispier tray into shelf position 4.
5. Select air fry mode. Set the temperature to 400 F and the timer for 20 minutes. Press start.
6. Stir cauliflower florets halfway through.
7. Serve and enjoy.

Nutritional Value (Amount per Serving):

- Calories 159
- Fat 14.2 g
- Carbohydrates 8.2 g
- Sugar 3.1 g
- Protein 2.8 g
- Cholesterol 0 mg

Crispy Eggplant

Preparation Time: 10 minutes
Cooking Time: 20 minutes
Serve: 4
Ingredients:

- 1 eggplant, cut into 1-inch pieces
- 1/2 tsp red pepper
- 1 tsp garlic powder
- 2 tbsp olive oil
- 1/2 tsp Italian seasoning
- 1 tsp paprika

Directions:

1. Add eggplant and remaining ingredients into the bowl and toss well.
2. Add eggplant to the crispier tray.
3. Place the drip tray below the bottom of the air fryer.
4. Insert the crispier tray into shelf position 4.
5. Select air fry mode. Set the temperature to 375 F and the timer for 20 minutes. Press start.
6. Stir eggplant pieces halfway through.
7. Serve and enjoy.

Nutritional Value (Amount per Serving):

- Calories 99
- Fat 7.5 g
- Carbohydrates 8.7 g
- Sugar 4.5 g
- Protein 1.5 g
- Cholesterol 0 mg

Chapter 7: Snacks & Appetizers

Cheesy Artichoke Spinach Dip

Preparation Time: 10 minutes
Cooking Time: 20 minutes
Serve: 8
Ingredients:

- 8 oz cream cheese, softened
- 6 oz frozen spinach, thawed & squeezed
- 14 oz can artichoke hearts, drain & chopped
- 1/2 cup mozzarella cheese, shredded
- 2/3 cup parmesan cheese, shredded
- 1 tsp garlic, minced
- 1/4 cup mayonnaise
- 1/4 cup sour cream

Directions:

1. Spray a 1-quart baking dish with cooking spray and set aside.
2. Add all ingredients into the large mixing bowl and mix until well combined.
3. Pour mixture into the prepared baking dish.
4. Select bake mode. Set the temperature to 350 F and the timer for 20 minutes. Press start.
5. Let the air fryer preheat then insert the pizza rack into shelf position 5.
6. Place baking dish on the pizza rack and bake.
7. Serve and enjoy.

Nutritional Value (Amount per Serving):

- Calories 192
- Fat 15.9 g
- Carbohydrates 6.5 g
- Sugar 1 g
- Protein 6.8 g
- Cholesterol 43 mg

Goat Cheese Dip

Preparation Time: 10 minutes
Cooking Time: 20 minutes
Serve: 8
Ingredients:

- 12 oz goat cheese, crumbled
- 2 tsp rosemary, chopped
- 1 tsp red pepper flakes
- 5 garlic cloves, minced

- 2 tbsp olive oil
- 1/2 cup parmesan cheese, shredded
- 4 oz cream cheese
- 1/2 tsp salt

Directions:

1. Spray a baking dish with cooking spray and set aside.
2. Add all ingredients into the large bowl and mix until well combined.
3. Pour mixture into the prepared baking dish.
4. Select bake mode. Set the temperature to 400 F and the timer for 20 minutes. Press start.
5. Let the air fryer preheat then insert the pizza rack into shelf position 5.
6. Place baking dish on the pizza rack and bake.
7. Serve and enjoy.

Nutritional Value (Amount per Serving):

- Calories 294
- Fat 24.9 g
- Carbohydrates 2.4 g
- Sugar 1 g
- Protein 16 g
- Cholesterol 64 mg

Chicken Meatballs

Preparation Time: 10 minutes
Cooking Time: 25 minutes
Serve: 6
Ingredients:

- 1 egg
- 1 lb ground chicken
- 1/4 tsp red pepper flakes
- 1/4 tsp pepper
- 1/2 tsp dried oregano
- 1 tsp dried onion flakes
- 1 garlic clove, minced
- 2 tbsp olive oil
- 1 tbsp parsley, chopped
- 1/2 cup breadcrumbs
- 1/2 cup parmesan cheese, grated
- 1/2 tsp sea salt

Directions:

1. Add all ingredients into the mixing bowl and mix until well combined.
2. Make balls from the meat mixture and place them onto the parchment-lined baking sheet.
3. Select bake mode. Set the temperature to 400 F and the timer for 25 minutes. Press start.
4. Let the air fryer preheat then insert the pizza rack into shelf position 5.
5. Place baking sheet on the pizza rack and bake.

6. Serve and enjoy.

Nutritional Value (Amount per Serving):

- Calories 257
- Fat 13.1 g
- Carbohydrates 7.4 g
- Sugar 0.8 g
- Protein 26.5 g
- Cholesterol 100 mg

Blue Cheese Dip

Preparation Time: 10 minutes
Cooking Time: 15 minutes
Serve: 8
Ingredients:

- 8 oz cream cheese, softened
- 3 tbsp green onions, chopped
- 4 bacon slices, crumbled
- 1 tsp garlic powder
- 6 oz blue cheese, crumbled
- 1/3 cup mayonnaise

Directions:

1. Spray a baking dish with cooking spray and set aside.
2. Add all ingredients into the large bowl and mix until well combined.
3. Pour mixture into the prepared baking dish.
4. Select bake mode. Set the temperature to 350 F and the timer for 15 minutes. Press start.
5. Let the air fryer preheat then insert the pizza rack into shelf position 5.
6. Place baking dish on the pizza rack and bake.
7. Serve and enjoy.

Nutritional Value (Amount per Serving):

- Calories 265
- Fat 23.2 g
- Carbohydrates 4.2 g
- Sugar 0.9 g
- Protein 10.4 g
- Cholesterol 60 mg

Baked Meatballs

Preparation Time: 10 minutes
Cooking Time: 30 minutes
Serve: 6
Ingredients:

- 1 egg
- 1/4 tsp pepper
- 1/2 tsp ground ginger
- 1 tsp garlic powder

- 1/2 cup breadcrumbs
- 1 lb ground chicken
- 1 tsp salt

Directions:

1. Add all ingredients into the mixing bowl and mix until well combined.
2. Make balls from the meat mixture and place them onto the parchment-lined baking sheet.
3. Select bake mode. Set the temperature to 400 F and the timer for 30 minutes. Press start.
4. Let the air fryer preheat then insert the pizza rack into shelf position 5.
5. Place baking sheet on the pizza rack and bake.
6. Serve and enjoy.

Nutritional Value (Amount per Serving):

- Calories 192
- Fat 6.8 g
- Carbohydrates 7.1 g
- Sugar 0.7 g
- Protein 24.1 g
- Cholesterol 95 mg

Cheesy Beef Dip

Preparation Time: 10 minutes
Cooking Time: 25 minutes
Serve: 12
Ingredients:

- 1 lb corned beef, diced
- 1/4 cup thousand island dressing
- 3/4 cup mayonnaise
- 14 oz can sauerkraut, drained
- 8 oz Swiss cheese, shredded
- Pepper
- Salt

Directions:

1. Spray a baking dish with cooking spray and set aside.
2. Add all ingredients into the large bowl and mix until well combined.
3. Pour mixture into the prepared baking dish.
4. Select bake mode. Set the temperature to 400 F and the timer for 25 minutes. Press start.
5. Let the air fryer preheat then insert the pizza rack into shelf position 5.
6. Place baking dish on the pizza rack and bake.
7. Serve and enjoy.

Nutritional Value (Amount per Serving):

- Calories 218
- Fat 16.7 g

- Carbohydrates 6.5 g
- Sugar 3.2 g
- Protein 10.3 g
- Cholesterol 46 mg

Tasty Carrot Fries

Preparation Time: 10 minutes
Cooking Time: 15 minutes
Serve: 2
Ingredients:

- 2 medium carrots, cut into fries shape
- 2 tbsp lemon-herb seasoning
- 2 tbsp olive oil

Directions:
1. Add carrot fries, seasoning, and oil into the bowl and toss well.
2. Spread carrot fries into the crisper tray.
3. Place the drip tray below the bottom of the air fryer.
4. Insert the crispier tray into shelf position 4.
5. Select air fry mode. Set the temperature to 350 F and the timer for 15 minutes. Press start.

Nutritional Value (Amount per Serving):
- Calories 145
- Fat 14 g
- Carbohydrates 6 g
- Sugar 3 g
- Protein 0.5 g
- Cholesterol 0 mg

Zucchini Chips

Preparation Time: 10 minutes
Cooking Time: 10 minutes
Serve: 2
Ingredients:

- 2 zucchini, cut into 1/4-inch thick slices
- 1 1/2 tsp garlic & herb seasoning
- 2 tsp olive oil
- 1/2 tsp sea salt

Directions:
1. Add zucchini slices, seasoning, oil, and salt into the mixing bowl and toss well.
2. Arrange zucchini slices into the crisper tray.
3. Place the drip tray below the bottom of the air fryer.
4. Insert the crispier tray into shelf position 4.

5. Select air fry mode. Set the temperature to 350 F and the timer for 10 minutes. Press start.
6. Serve and enjoy.

Nutritional Value (Amount per Serving):

- Calories 71
- Fat 5 g
- Carbohydrates 6.6 g
- Sugar 3.4 g
- Protein 2.4 g
- Cholesterol 0 mg

Crispy Potato Wedges

Preparation Time: 10 minutes
Cooking Time: 20 minutes
Serve: 4
Ingredients:

- 2 potatoes, cut into wedges
- 2 tbsp taco potato seasoning
- 2 tbsp olive oil
- 1 tbsp sea salt

Directions:

1. Add potato wedges and remaining ingredients into the mixing bowl and toss well.
2. Arrange potato wedges into the crisper tray.
3. Place the drip tray below the bottom of the air fryer.
4. Insert the crispier tray into shelf position 4.
5. Select air fry mode. Set the temperature to 400 F and the timer for 20 minutes. Press start.
6. Turn potato wedges after 10 minutes.
7. Serve and enjoy.

Nutritional Value (Amount per Serving):

- Calories 141
- Fat 7.4 g
- Carbohydrates 17.7 g
- Sugar 1.3 g
- Protein 1.9 g
- Cholesterol 0 mg

Sweet Potato Fries

Preparation Time: 10 minutes
Cooking Time: 16 minutes
Serve: 2
Ingredients:

- 1 sweet potato, peel and cut into strips
- 1 tsp cayenne
- 1 tbsp olive oil
- 1 tbsp sea salt

Directions:

1. Add sweet potato strips and remaining ingredients into the mixing bowl and toss well.
2. Arrange sweet potato strips into the crisper tray.
3. Place the drip tray below the bottom of the air fryer.
4. Insert the crispier tray into shelf position 4.
5. Select air fry mode. Set the temperature to 400 F and the timer for 16 minutes. Press start.
6. Turn sweet potato strips after 8 minutes.
7. Serve and enjoy.

Nutritional Value (Amount per Serving):

- Calories 114
- Fat 7.3 g
- Carbohydrates 12.3 g
- Sugar 3.8 g
- Protein 1.3 g
- Cholesterol 0 mg

Quick & Tasty Chickpeas

Preparation Time: 10 minutes
Cooking Time: 16 minutes
Serve: 4

Ingredients:

- 15 oz can chickpeas, drained
- 1/2 tsp dry mustard
- 1/2 tsp garlic powder
- 1/2 tsp celery salt
- 1 tsp brown sugar
- 1 1/2 tsp paprika
- 1/4 tsp pepper

Directions:

1. Add chickpeas and remaining ingredients into the mixing bowl and toss well.
2. Spread chickpeas in a crispier tray.
3. Place the drip tray below the bottom of the air fryer.
4. Insert the crispier tray into shelf position 4.
5. Select air fry mode. Set the temperature to 390 F and the timer for 16 minutes. Press start.
6. Stir chickpeas after 8 minutes.
7. Serve and enjoy.

Nutritional Value (Amount per Serving):

- Calories 135
- Fat 1.4 g
- Carbohydrates 25.7 g
- Sugar 0.9 g
- Protein 5.6 g
- Cholesterol 0 mg

Spicy Cashews

Preparation Time: 10 minutes
Cooking Time: 8 minutes
Serve: 2
Ingredients:

- 1 cup cashews
- 1 tsp butter, melted
- 1/2 tsp pepper
- 1/4 tsp red chili powder
- 1/4 tsp paprika
- Salt

Directions:

1. Add cashews and remaining ingredients into the mixing bowl and toss well.
2. Spread cashews in the crisper tray.
3. Place the drip tray below the bottom of the air fryer.
4. Insert the crispier tray into shelf position 4.
5. Select air fry mode. Set the temperature to 350 F and the timer for 8 minutes. Press start.
6. Stir cashews after 5 minutes.
7. Serve and enjoy.

Nutritional Value (Amount per Serving):

- Calories 413
- Fat 33.8 g
- Carbohydrates 23.1 g
- Sugar 3.5 g
- Protein 10.7 g
- Cholesterol 5 mg

Ranch Potatoes

Preparation Time: 10 minutes
Cooking Time: 20 minutes
Serve: 2
Ingredients:

- 1/2 lb baby potatoes, wash and cut in half
- 1/4 tsp parsley
- 1/2 tbsp olive oil
- 1/4 tsp dill
- 1/4 tsp chives

- 1/4 tsp paprika
- 1/4 tsp onion powder
- 1/4 tsp garlic powder
- Salt

Directions:

1. Add all ingredients into the bowl and toss well.
2. Spread potatoes in a crispier tray.
3. Place the drip tray below the bottom of the air fryer.
4. Insert the crispier tray into shelf position 4.
5. Select air fry mode. Set the temperature to 400 F and the timer for 20 minutes. Press start.
6. Stir potatoes after 10 minutes.
7. Serve and enjoy.

Nutritional Value (Amount per Serving):

- Calories 99
- Fat 3.7 g
- Carbohydrates 14.8 g
- Sugar 0.2 g
- Protein 3.1 g
- Cholesterol 0 mg

Salsa Cheese Dip

Preparation Time: 10 minutes
Cooking Time: 30 minutes
Serve: 10
Ingredients:

- 16 oz cream cheese, softened
- 1/2 cup hot salsa
- 3 cups cheddar cheese, shredded
- 1 cup sour cream

Directions:

1. Spray a baking dish with cooking spray and set aside.
2. Add all ingredients into the large bowl and mix until well combined.
3. Pour mixture into the prepared baking dish.
4. Select bake mode. Set the temperature to 350 F and the timer for 30 minutes. Press start.
5. Let the air fryer preheat then insert the pizza rack into shelf position 5.
6. Place baking dish on the pizza rack and bake.
7. Serve and enjoy.

Nutritional Value (Amount per Serving):

- Calories 348
- Fat 31.8 g
- Carbohydrates 3.4 g
- Sugar 0.7 g
- Protein 12.8 g
- Cholesterol 96 mg

Delicious Onion Dip

Preparation Time: 10 minutes
Cooking Time: 40 minutes
Serve: 8

Ingredients:

- 1 1/2 onions, chopped
- 1 1/2 cup mayonnaise
- 1/2 tsp garlic powder
- 1 1/2 cup Swiss cheese, shredded
- 1 cup mozzarella cheese, shredded
- 1 cup cheddar cheese, shredded
- Pepper
- Salt

Directions:

1. Spray a baking dish with cooking spray and set aside.
2. Add all ingredients into the large bowl and mix until well combined.
3. Pour mixture into the prepared baking dish.
4. Select bake mode. Set the temperature to 350 F and the timer for 40 minutes. Press start.
5. Let the air fryer preheat then insert the pizza rack into shelf position 5.
6. Place baking dish on the pizza rack and bake.
7. Serve and enjoy.

Nutritional Value (Amount per Serving):

- Calories 325
- Fat 25.7 g
- Carbohydrates 14 g
- Sugar 4.1 g
- Protein 10.6 g
- Cholesterol 47 mg

Chapter 8: Dehydrate

Kiwi Slices

Preparation Time: 10 minutes
Cooking Time: 12 hours
Serve: 6
Ingredients:
- 6 kiwis, peeled and cut into 1/4-inch thick slices

Directions:
1. Place the drip tray below the bottom of the air fryer.
2. Insert the crisper tray into position 2 then insert the pizza rack into position 5.
3. Place kiwi slices on the crisper tray and pizza rack.
4. Select dehydrate mode. Set the temperature to 135 F and the timer for 12 hours. Press start.
5. Store in an air-tight container.

Nutritional Value (Amount per Serving):
- Calories 46
- Fat 0.4 g
- Carbohydrates 11.1 g
- Sugar 6.8 g
- Protein 0.9 g
- Cholesterol 0 mg

Dehydrated Raspberries

Preparation Time: 10 minutes
Cooking Time: 18 hours
Serve: 4
Ingredients:
- 4 cups raspberries, wash and dry
- 1/4 cup fresh lemon juice

Directions:
1. Place the drip tray below the bottom of the air fryer.
2. Insert the crisper tray into position 2 then insert the pizza rack into position 5.
3. Arrange raspberries on the crisper tray and pizza rack.
4. Select dehydrate mode. Set the temperature to 135 F and the timer for 18 hours. Press start.
5. Store in an air-tight container.

Nutritional Value (Amount per Serving):
- Calories 68
- Fat 0.9 g

- Carbohydrates 15 g
- Sugar 5.8 g
- Protein 1.6 g
- Cholesterol 0 mg

Strawberry Slices

Preparation Time: 10 minutes
Cooking Time: 12 hours
Serve: 6
Ingredients:

- 3 cups strawberries, cut into 1/4-inch thick slices

Directions:

1. Place the drip tray below the bottom of the air fryer.
2. Insert the crisper tray into position 2 then insert the pizza rack into position 5.
3. Arrange strawberry slices on the crisper tray and pizza rack.
4. Select dehydrate mode. Set the temperature to 135 F and the timer for 12 hours. Press start.
5. Store dried strawberries in an air-tight container.

Nutritional Value (Amount per Serving):

- Calories 23
- Fat 0.2 g
- Carbohydrates 5.5 g
- Sugar 3.5 g
- Protein 0.5 g
- Cholesterol 0 mg

Green Apple Slices

Preparation Time: 10 minutes
Cooking Time: 8 hours
Serve: 5
Ingredients:

- 4 green apples, cored & cut into 8-inch thick slices
- 1/2 fresh lime juice

Directions:

1. Place the drip tray below the bottom of the air fryer.
2. Insert the crisper tray into position 2 then insert the pizza rack into position 5.
3. Add apple slices and lime juice in a bowl and toss well and set aside for 5 minutes.
4. Arrange apple slices on the crisper tray and pizza rack.
5. Select dehydrate mode. Set the temperature to 145 F and the timer for 8 hours. Press start.
6. Store in an air-tight container.

Nutritional Value (Amount per Serving):

- Calories 94
- Fat 0.3 g
- Carbohydrates 25 g
- Sugar 18.6 g
- Protein 0.5 g
- Cholesterol 0 mg

Peach Slices

Preparation Time: 10 minutes
Cooking Time: 8 hours
Serve: 6
Ingredients:

- 6 peaches, cut and remove pits and sliced
- 1/2 cup fresh lemon juice

Directions:

1. Place the drip tray below the bottom of the air fryer.
2. Insert the crisper tray into position 2 then insert the pizza rack into position 5.
3. Add lemon juice and peach slices into the bowl and toss well.
4. Arrange peach slices on the crisper tray and pizza rack.
5. Select dehydrate mode. Set the temperature to 135 F and the timer for 8 hours. Press start.

Nutritional Value (Amount per Serving):

- Calories 64
- Fat 0.6 g
- Carbohydrates 14.4 g
- Sugar 14.4 g
- Protein 1.6 g
- Cholesterol 0 mg

Banana Slices

Preparation Time: 10 minutes
Cooking Time: 8 hours
Serve: 4
Ingredients:

- 3 bananas, cut into 1/8-inch thick slices
- 1/2 cup fresh lemon juice

Directions:

1. Place the drip tray below the bottom of the air fryer.
2. Insert the crisper tray into position 2 then insert the pizza rack into position 5.
3. Add sliced bananas and lemon juice in a bowl and toss well.
4. Arrange banana slices on the crisper tray and pizza rack.

5. Select dehydrate mode. Set the temperature to 135 F and the timer for 8 hours. Press start.

Nutritional Value (Amount per Serving):

- Calories 86
- Fat 0.5 g
- Carbohydrates 20.9 g
- Sugar 11.5 g
- Protein 1.2 g
- Cholesterol 0 mg

Sweet Mango Slices

Preparation Time: 10 minutes
Cooking Time: 12 hours
Serve: 6
Ingredients:

- 4 mangoes, peel & cut into 1/4-inch thick slices
- 1 tbsp honey

Directions:

1. In a bowl, add mango slices and honey and toss well.
2. Place the drip tray below the bottom of the air fryer.
3. Insert the crisper tray into position 2 then insert the pizza rack into position 5.
4. Arrange mango slices on the crisper tray and pizza rack.
5. Select dehydrate mode. Set the temperature to 135 F and the timer for 12 hours. Press start.

Nutritional Value (Amount per Serving):

- Calories 145
- Fat 0.9 g
- Carbohydrates 36.4 g
- Sugar 33.5 g
- Protein 1.9 g
- Cholesterol 0 mg

Zucchini Chips

Preparation Time: 10 minutes
Cooking Time: 8 hours
Serve: 4
Ingredients:

- 2 medium zucchini, wash and cut into 1/4-inch slices
- 1/8 tsp cayenne pepper
- 1 tsp olive oil
- 1/8 tsp sea salt

Directions:

1. Add all ingredients into the bowl and toss well to coat.
2. Place the drip tray below the bottom of the air fryer.
3. Insert the crisper tray into position 2 then insert the pizza rack into position 5.
4. Arrange zucchini slices on the crisper tray and pizza rack.
5. Select dehydrate mode. Set the temperature to 135 F and the timer for 8 hours. Press start.
6. Store in an air-tight container.

Nutritional Value (Amount per Serving):
- Calories 26
- Fat 1.4 g
- Carbohydrates 3.3 g
- Sugar 1.7 g
- Protein 1.2 g
- Cholesterol 0 mg

Eggplant Slices

Preparation Time: 10 minutes
Cooking Time: 4 hours
Serve: 4

Ingredients:
- 2 medium eggplant, cut into 1/4-inch thick slices
- 1/4 tsp garlic powder
- 1 tsp paprika

Directions:
1. Place the drip tray below the bottom of the air fryer.
2. Insert the crisper tray into position 2 then insert the pizza rack into position 5.
3. Add all ingredients into the bowl and toss well.
4. Arrange eggplant slices on the crisper tray and pizza rack.
5. Select dehydrate mode. Set the temperature to 145 F and the timer for 4 hours. Press start.
6. Store in an air-tight container.

Nutritional Value (Amount per Serving):
- Calories 59
- Fat 0.5 g
- Carbohydrates 13.9 g
- Sugar 7 g
- Protein 2.4 g
- Cholesterol 0 mg

Sweet Potato Slices

Preparation Time: 10 minutes
Cooking Time: 12 hours
Serve: 2

Ingredients:

- 2 sweet potatoes, peel and sliced thinly
- 1/8 tsp ground cinnamon
- 1 tsp olive oil
- Salt

Directions:

1. Place the drip tray below the bottom of the air fryer.
2. Insert the crisper tray into position 2 then insert the pizza rack into position 5.
3. Add sweet potato slices in a bowl.
4. Add cinnamon, oil, and salt and toss well.
5. Arrange sweet potato slices on the crisper tray and pizza rack.
6. Select dehydrate mode. Set the temperature to 125 F and the timer for 12 hours. Press start.
7. Store in an air-tight container.

Nutritional Value (Amount per Serving):

- Calories 138
- Fat 2.5 g
- Carbohydrates 28 g
- Sugar 0.5 g
- Protein 1.5 g
- Cholesterol 0 mg

Salmon Jerky

Preparation Time: 10 minutes
Cooking Time: 4 hours
Serve: 6

Ingredients:

- 1 lb salmon, cut into 1/4-inch slices
- 1 tbsp molasses
- 1/2 cup soy sauce
- 1/2 tsp liquid smoke
- 1 tsp pepper
- 1 tbsp fresh lemon juice

Directions:

1. Place the drip tray below the bottom of the air fryer.
2. Insert the crisper tray into position 2 then insert the pizza rack into position 5.
3. In a bowl, mix liquid smoke, pepper, lemon juice, molasses, and soy sauce.
4. Add salmon slices into the bowl and mix well. Cover and place in the refrigerator overnight.
5. Strain salmon slices and pat dry with a paper towel.
6. Arrange salmon slices on the crisper tray and pizza rack.

7. Select dehydrate mode. Set the temperature to 145 F and the timer for 4 hours. Press start.

Nutritional Value (Amount per Serving):

- Calories 122
- Fat 4.7 g
- Carbohydrates 4.4 g
- Sugar 2.3 g
- Protein 16.1 g
- Cholesterol 33 mg

Chicken Jerky

Preparation Time: 10 minutes
Cooking Time: 7 hours
Serve: 4
Ingredients:

- 1 lb chicken tenders, boneless, skinless and cut into 1/4-inch slices
- 1/2 tsp garlic powder
- 1 tsp lemon juice
- 1/2 cup soy sauce
- 1/4 tsp ground ginger
- 1/4 tsp pepper

Directions:

1. Place the drip tray below the bottom of the air fryer.
2. Insert the crisper tray into position 2 then insert the pizza rack into position 5.
3. Mix all ingredients except chicken into the zip-lock bag.
4. Add chicken and seal bag. Place in refrigerator for 30 minutes.
5. Arrange marinated chicken slices on the crisper tray and pizza rack.
6. Select dehydrate mode. Set the temperature to 145 F and the timer for 7 hours. Press start.

Nutritional Value (Amount per Serving):

- Calories 235
- Fat 8.4 g
- Carbohydrates 2.9 g
- Sugar 0.7 g
- Protein 34.9 g
- Cholesterol 101 mg

Spicy Almonds

Preparation Time: 10 minutes
Cooking Time: 10 hours
Serve: 4
Ingredients:

- 2 cups almonds, soaked in water for overnight
- 1/2 tsp chili powder
- 1 tbsp olive oil

Directions:
1. Place the drip tray below the bottom of the air fryer.
2. Insert the crisper tray into position 2 then insert the pizza rack into position 5.
3. Toss almonds with oil and chili powder and spread on the crisper tray and pizza rack.
4. Select dehydrate mode. Set the temperature to 125 F and the timer for 10 hours. Press start.

Nutritional Value (Amount per Serving):
- Calories 306
- Fat 27.3 g
- Carbohydrates 10.4 g
- Sugar 2 g
- Protein 10.1 g
- Cholesterol 0 mg

Beet Slices

Preparation Time: 10 minutes
Cooking Time: 10 hours
Serve: 2

Ingredients:
- 2 beet, sliced thinly
- Salt

Directions:
1. Place the drip tray below the bottom of the air fryer.
2. Insert the crisper tray into position 2 then insert the pizza rack into position 5.
3. Season beet slices with salt and arrange on the crisper tray and pizza rack.
4. Select dehydrate mode. Set the temperature to 135 F and the timer for 10 hours. Press start.

Nutritional Value (Amount per Serving):
- Calories 44
- Fat 0.2 g
- Carbohydrates 10 g
- Sugar 8 g
- Protein 1.7 g
- Cholesterol 0 mg

Broccoli Florets

Preparation Time: 10 minutes
Cooking Time: 12 hours
Serve: 6

Ingredients:

- 1 lb broccoli florets
- Pepper
- Salt

Directions:

1. Place the drip tray below the bottom of the air fryer.
2. Insert the crisper tray into position 2 then insert the pizza rack into position 5.
3. Season broccoli florets with pepper and salt and arrange on the crisper tray and pizza rack.
4. Select dehydrate mode. Set the temperature to 115 F and the timer for 12 hours. Press start.

Nutritional Value (Amount per Serving):

- Calories 26
- Fat 0.3 g
- Carbohydrates 5 g
- Sugar 1.3 g
- Protein 2.1 g
- Cholesterol 0 mg

Chapter 9: Desserts

Choco Peanut Butter Cookies

Preparation Time: 10 minutes
Cooking Time: 8 minutes
Serve: 36
Ingredients:

- 1 egg
- 3/4 tsp baking soda
- 1 1/4 cups all-purpose flour
- 1 tsp vanilla
- 3 tbsp milk
- 1 1/2 cups light brown sugar
- 3/4 cup creamy peanut butter
- 1/2 cup cocoa powder
- 1/2 cup butter
- 3/4 tsp salt

Directions:

1. In a large bowl, mix together milk, vanilla, butter, brown sugar, and peanut butter. Add egg and beat until well blended.
2. In a bowl, mix flour, cocoa powder, salt, and baking soda.
3. Add flour mixture into the milk mixture and mix until well blended.
4. Make cookies from mixture and place on a parchment-lined baking sheet.
5. Select bake mode. Set the temperature to 375 F and the timer for 8 minutes. Press start.
6. Let the air fryer preheat then insert the pizza rack into shelf position 5.
7. Place baking sheet on the pizza rack and bake cookies in batches.
8. Serve and enjoy.

Nutritional Value (Amount per Serving):

- Calories 98
- Fat 5.6 g
- Carbohydrates 11 g
- Sugar 6.5 g
- Protein 2.3 g
- Cholesterol 11 mg

Choco Chip Cookie Bars

Preparation Time: 10 minutes
Cooking Time: 30 minutes
Serve: 12
Ingredients:

- 2 eggs
- 1 1/2 cups chocolate chips
- 1/2 tsp baking soda
- 1 1/2 cup all-purpose flour

- 1 tsp vanilla
- 1/2 cup sugar
- 1/2 cup brown sugar
- 1 stick butter, softened
- 1/2 tsp salt

Directions:

1. Line 8*8-inch baking dish with parchment paper and set aside.
2. In a large bowl, beat sugar, butter, and brown sugar until fluffy.
3. Add eggs, vanilla, and salt and beat until well blended.
4. Add baking soda and flour and mix until well combined. Add chocolate chips and mix well.
5. Pour mixture into the prepared baking dish and spread well.
6. Select bake mode. Set the temperature to 350 F and the timer for 30 minutes. Press start.
7. Let the air fryer preheat then insert the pizza rack into shelf position 5.
8. Place baking dish on the pizza rack and bake cookie bar.
9. Slice and serve.

Nutritional Value (Amount per Serving):

- Calories 302
- Fat 14.8 g
- Carbohydrates 38.8 g
- Sugar 25.2 g
- Protein 4.2 g
- Cholesterol 52 mg

Raspberry Muffins

Preparation Time: 10 minutes
Cooking Time: 20 minutes
Serve: 12
Ingredients:

- 1 egg
- 1 cup raspberries
- 1/2 cup canola oil
- 6 oz yogurt
- 1/2 tsp baking soda
- 1 tsp baking powder
- 1/3 cup sugar
- 1 3/4 cups all-purpose flour
- 1/2 tsp salt

Directions:

1. Line muffin pan with cupcake liners and set aside.
2. In a bowl, mix together all dry ingredients.
3. In a small bowl, whisk together egg, oil, and yogurt.
4. Add egg mixture and raspberries into the dry mixture and mix until well blended.
5. Spoon mixture into the prepared muffin pan.

6. Select bake mode. Set the temperature to 400 F and the timer for 20 minutes. Press start.
7. Let the air fryer preheat then insert the pizza rack into shelf position 5.
8. Place muffin pan on the pizza rack and bake.
9. Serve and enjoy.

Nutritional Value (Amount per Serving):

- Calories 189
- Fat 9.9 g
- Carbohydrates 21.9 g
- Sugar 7.1 g
- Protein 3.3 g
- Cholesterol 15 mg

Moist Pumpkin Muffins

Preparation Time: 10 minutes
Cooking Time: 20 minutes
Serve: 16
Ingredients:

- 2 eggs
- 1 tsp cinnamon
- 1 tbsp pumpkin pie spice
- 1/3 cup vegetable oil
- 1 tbsp vanilla
- 15 oz can pumpkin puree
- 1 tsp baking soda
- 2 tsp baking powder
- 1 cup of sugar
- 1/2 cup brown sugar
- 8 oz yogurt
- 2 cups all-purpose flour
- 1/2 tsp salt

Directions:
1. Line muffin pan with cupcake liners and set aside.
2. In a mixing bowl, mix flour, pumpkin pie spice, baking powder, cinnamon, salt, and baking soda.
3. In a separate bowl, beat eggs, pumpkin, sugar, oil, brown sugar, and yogurt until well blended.
4. Add flour mixture into the egg mixture and stir until well combined.
5. Spoon mixture into the prepared muffin pan.
6. Select bake mode. Set the temperature to 325 F and the timer for 20 minutes. Press start.
7. Let the air fryer preheat then insert the pizza rack into shelf position 5.
8. Place muffin pan on the pizza rack and bake.
9. Serve and enjoy.

Nutritional Value (Amount per Serving):

- Calories 223
- Fat 5.5 g
- Carbohydrates 40 g
- Sugar 21.9 g
- Protein 4.1 g
- Cholesterol 21 mg

Easy Nutella Brownies

Preparation Time: 10 minutes
Cooking Time: 20 minutes
Serve: 16
Ingredients:

- 2 eggs
- 1/2 cup all-purpose flour
- 1 1/4 cups Nutella

Directions:

1. Line 8*8-inch baking dish with parchment paper and set aside.
2. In a bowl, mix eggs and Nutella until smooth.
3. Add flour and mix until well combined.
4. Pour mixture into the prepared 8*8-inch baking dish.
5. Select bake mode. Set the temperature to 350 F and the timer for 20 minutes. Press start.
6. Let the air fryer preheat then insert the pizza rack into shelf position 5.
7. Place baking dish on the pizza rack and bake.
8. Slice and serve.

Nutritional Value (Amount per Serving):

- Calories 93
- Fat 4.3 g
- Carbohydrates 11.5 g
- Sugar 4.5 g
- Protein 2.3 g
- Cholesterol 36 mg

Baked Donuts

Preparation Time: 10 minutes
Cooking Time: 15 minutes
Serve: 12
Ingredients:

- 2 eggs
- 1 cup all-purpose flour
- 1/2 tsp vanilla
- 1 tsp baking powder
- 3/4 cup sugar
- 1/2 cup buttermilk
- 1/4 cup olive oil
- 1/2 tsp salt

Directions:

1. Spray donut pan with cooking spray and set aside.
2. In a bowl, mix together eggs, vanilla, baking powder, sugar, buttermilk, oil, and salt until well combined.
3. Add flour and mix until well combined.
4. Pour mixture into the prepared donut pan.
5. Select bake mode. Set the temperature to 350 F and the timer for 15 minutes. Press start.
6. Let the air fryer preheat then insert the pizza rack into shelf position 5.
7. Place donut pan on the pizza rack and bake.
8. Serve and enjoy.

Nutritional Value (Amount per Serving):

- Calories 136
- Fat 5.1 g
- Carbohydrates 21.2 g
- Sugar 13.1 g
- Protein 2.3 g
- Cholesterol 28 mg

Blueberry Muffins

Preparation Time: 10 minutes
Cooking Time: 18 minutes
Serve: 24

Ingredients:

- 2 eggs
- 2 cups blueberries
- 6 tsp baking powder
- 2/3 cup sugar
- 2 cups whole wheat flour
- 2 cups all-purpose flour
- 2 cups almond milk
- 2/3 cup olive oil
- 1 tsp salt

Directions:

1. Line muffin pan with cupcake liners and set aside.
2. In a bowl, mix flours, blueberries, baking powder, sugar, and salt.
3. In a small bowl, whisk eggs with oil and milk.
4. Pour egg mixture into the flour mixture and mix until well combined.
5. Pour mixture into the prepared muffin pan.
6. Select bake mode. Set the temperature to 400 F and the timer for 18 minutes. Press start.
7. Let the air fryer preheat then insert the pizza rack into shelf position 5.
8. Place muffin pan on the pizza rack and bake.

9. Serve and enjoy.

Nutritional Value (Amount per Serving):

- Calories 204
- Fat 11 g
- Carbohydrates 24.9 g
- Sugar 7.5 g
- Protein 3.2 g
- Cholesterol 14 mg

Delicious Date Brownies

Preparation Time: 10 minutes
Cooking Time: 20 minutes
Serve: 16

Ingredients:

- 1 cup dates, pitted
- 1/2 tsp baking powder
- 1/2 cup cocoa powder
- 3/4 cup almond flour
- 2 tsp vanilla
- 3 tbsp honey
- 3/4 cup hot water
- Pinch of sea salt

Directions:

1. Add dates and hot water to a bowl and let it sit for 10 minutes.
2. Drain dates and add into the food processor and process until smooth.
3. Add vanilla, honey, cocoa powder, almond flour, and salt into the food processor and process until smooth.
4. Pour mixture into the 8*8-inch greased pan.
5. Select bake mode. Set the temperature to 350 F and the timer for 20 minutes. Press start.
6. Let the air fryer preheat then insert the pizza rack into shelf position 5.
7. Place baking pan on the pizza rack and cook.
8. Slice and serve.

Nutritional Value (Amount per Serving):

- Calories 59
- Fat 1.1 g
- Carbohydrates 13.5 g
- Sugar 10.5 g
- Protein 1.1 g
- Cholesterol 0 mg

Baked Pears

Preparation Time: 10 minutes
Cooking Time: 25 minutes
Serve: 4

Ingredients:

- 4 pears, cut in half & core
- 1/2 cup maple syrup
- 1 tsp vanilla
- 1/4 tsp ground cinnamon

Directions:

1. Line baking sheet with parchment paper and set aside.
2. Arrange pears on the prepared baking sheet and sprinkle with cinnamon.
3. In a small bowl, mix maple syrup and vanilla. Reserved 2 tbsp of maple syrup.
4. Drizzle remaining maple syrup over pears.
5. Select bake mode. Set the temperature to 375 F and the timer for 25 minutes. Press start.
6. Let the air fryer preheat then insert the pizza rack into shelf position 5.
7. Place baking sheet on the pizza rack and cook.
8. Drizzle remaining maple syrup over pears.
9. Serve and enjoy.

Nutritional Value (Amount per Serving):

- Calories 227
- Fat 0.4 g
- Carbohydrates 58.5 g
- Sugar 44 g
- Protein 0.8 g
- Cholesterol 0 mg

Pumpkin Choco Chip Bread

Preparation Time: 10 minutes
Cooking Time: 35 minutes
Serve: 8

Ingredients:

- 2 eggs
- 1 tsp pumpkin pie spice
- 1 tsp baking powder
- 1/4 cup Swerve
- 1/4 cup flax seed meal
- 1/4 cup chocolate chips
- 1/2 cup pumpkin puree
- 1/4 cup coconut flour
- 1/4 tsp sea salt

Directions:

1. Spray a loaf pan with cooking spray and set aside.
2. Add all dry ingredients into the bowl and mix well. Set aside.
3. In a separate bowl, whisk together pumpkin puree and eggs.
4. Pour wet ingredients mixture into the dry ingredients and mix well.
5. Pour batter into the prepared loaf pan.

6. Select bake mode. Set the temperature to 350 F and the timer for 35 minutes. Press start.
7. Let the air fryer preheat then insert the pizza rack into shelf position 5.
8. Place loaf pan on the pizza rack and cook.
9. Slice and serve.

Nutritional Value (Amount per Serving):

- Calories 84
- Fat 4.2 g
- Carbohydrates 8.5 g
- Sugar 3.4 g
- Protein 3.1 g
- Cholesterol 42 mg

Chocolate Muffins

Preparation Time: 10 minutes
Cooking Time: 20 minutes
Serve: 12
Ingredients:

- 4 eggs
- 1 tsp vanilla
- 1/4 cup butter
- 1 oz chocolate chips
- 1 oz chocolate, chopped
- 1/4 cup cocoa powder
- 1/2 cup almond flour
- 1 tsp baking powder
- 1/4 cup heavy cream
- 1/4 cup erythritol
- Pinch of salt

Directions:

1. Line muffin pan with cupcake liners and set aside.
2. In a bowl, mix almond flour, erythritol, baking powder, cocoa powder, and salt.
3. In a separate bowl, beat together butter and heavy cream.
4. Add vanilla and eggs and beat until just combined.
5. Add almond flour mixture to the egg mixture and mix until well combined.
6. Add chocolate and chocolate chips and stir well.
7. Pour batter into a prepared muffin pan.
8. Select bake mode. Set the temperature to 350 F and the timer for 20 minutes. Press start.
9. Let the air fryer preheat then insert the pizza rack into shelf position 5.
10. Place muffin pan on the pizza rack and cook.
11. Serve and enjoy.

Nutritional Value (Amount per Serving):

- Calories 101
- Fat 8.4 g

- Carbohydrates 4.5 g
- Sugar 2.7 g
- Protein 2.9 g
- Cholesterol 69 mg

Delicious Chocolate Cake

Preparation Time: 10 minutes
Cooking Time: 30 minutes
Serve: 12
Ingredients:

- 5 eggs
- 1/2 cup almond flour
- 10 oz butter, melted
- 1 1/2 cup erythritol
- 10 oz chocolate, melted
- Pinch of salt

Directions:

1. Grease spring-form cake pan with butter and set aside.
2. In a mixing bowl, beat eggs until foamy.
3. Add sweetener and stir well.
4. Add melted butter, chocolate, almond flour, and salt and stir to combine.
5. Pour batter into the prepared cake pan.
6. Select bake mode. Set the temperature to 350 F and the timer for 30 minutes. Press start.
7. Let the air fryer preheat then insert the pizza rack into shelf position 5.
8. Place cake pan on the pizza rack and cook.
9. Slice and serve.

Nutritional Value (Amount per Serving):

- Calories 329
- Fat 28.6 g
- Carbohydrates 14.4 g
- Sugar 12.4 g
- Protein 4.6 g
- Cholesterol 124 mg

Pound Cake

Preparation Time: 10 minutes
Cooking Time: 35 minutes
Serve: 8
Ingredients:

- 5 eggs
- 1 tsp orange extract
- 1 cup Splenda
- 4 oz cream cheese, softened
- 1/2 cup butter, softened
- 1 tsp baking powder

- 6.5 oz almond flour
- 1 tsp vanilla extract

Directions:

1. Spray a 9-inch cake pan with cooking spray and set aside.
2. Add all ingredients into the mixing bowl and mix until the mixture is fluffy and thick.
3. Pour batter into the prepared cake pan.
4. Select bake mode. Set the temperature to 350 F and the timer for 35 minutes. Press start.
5. Let the air fryer preheat then insert the pizza rack into shelf position 5.
6. Place cake pan on the pizza rack and cook.
7. Remove cake from oven and set aside to cool completely.
8. Slice and serve.

Nutritional Value (Amount per Serving):

- Calories 444
- Fat 30.6 g
- Carbohydrates 29.9 g
- Sugar 25.2 g
- Protein 9.5 g
- Cholesterol 148 mg

Chocolate Cookies

Preparation Time: 10 minutes
Cooking Time: 10 minutes
Serve: 20

Ingredients:

- 2 tbsp chocolate protein powder
- 3 tbsp ground chia
- 1 cup almond flour
- 1 cup almond butter

Directions:

1. Line baking sheet with parchment paper and set aside.
2. In a large bowl, add all ingredients and mix until combined.
3. Make cookies from mixture and place on a prepared baking sheet.
4. Select bake mode. Set the temperature to 350 F and the timer for 10 minutes. Press start.
5. Let the air fryer preheat then insert the pizza rack into shelf position 5.
6. Place baking sheet on the pizza rack and bake.
7. Remove from oven and set aside to cool completely.
8. Serve and enjoy.

Nutritional Value (Amount per Serving):

- Calories 26
- Fat 1.5 g

- Carbohydrates 1.1 g
- Sugar 0.3 g
- Protein 2.6 g
- Cholesterol 4 mg

Blueberry Brownie

Preparation Time: 10 minutes
Cooking Time: 25 minutes
Serve: 12
Ingredients:

- 3 eggs
- 1 tbsp coffee
- 1 tbsp cinnamon
- 4 tbsp cocoa powder
- 1 cup coconut cream, melted
- 1/2 cup honey
- 1 cup fresh blueberries
- 1/2 tsp baking soda
- 2 tsp vanilla extract
- Pinch of salt

Directions:

1. In a bowl, whisk together eggs, baking soda, salt, vanilla, coffee, cinnamon, cocoa powder, and honey.
2. Add blueberries into the egg mixture and fold well.
3. Pour mixture into the greased baking pan.
4. Select bake mode. Set the temperature to 325 F and the timer for 25 minutes. Press start.
5. Let the air fryer preheat then insert the pizza rack into shelf position 5.
6. Place baking pan on the pizza rack and bake.
7. Drizzle coconut cream over brownie.
8. Slice and serve.

Nutritional Value (Amount per Serving):

- Calories 119
- Fat 6.2 g
- Carbohydrates 16.1 g
- Sugar 13.7 g
- Protein 2.3 g
- Cholesterol 41 mg

Chapter 10: 30-Day Meal Plan

Day 1

Breakfast- Greek Egg Muffins

Lunch- Baked Balsamic Chicken

Dinner- Slow Cook Flank Steak

Day 2

Breakfast- Spinach Pepper Egg Muffins

Lunch- Tasty Smothered Chicken

Dinner- Steak & Mushrooms

Day 3

Breakfast- Healthy Spinach Frittata

Lunch- Parmesan Chicken Breasts

Dinner- Air Fryer Steak

Day 4

Breakfast- Quinoa Veggie Egg Muffins

Lunch- Rosemary Chicken & Potatoes

Dinner- Tasty Beef Fajitas

Day 5

Breakfast- Tomato Spinach Egg Muffins

Lunch- Stuffed Peppers

Dinner- Juicy Pork Chops

Day 6

Breakfast- Healthy Artichoke Frittata

Lunch- Scallop Gratin

Dinner- Honey Garlic Pork Chops

Day 7

Breakfast- Healthy Breakfast Muffins

Lunch- Dijon Salmon

Dinner- Tender Pork Loin

Day 8

Breakfast- Pumpkin Steel Cut Oats

Lunch- Flavorful Potato Casserole

Dinner- Mustard Honey Pork Chops

Day 9

Breakfast- Healthy Almond Oatmeal

Lunch- Cajun Salmon

Dinner- Herb Pork Chops

Day 10

Breakfast- Blueberry Oats

Lunch- Baked Lemon Pepper Basa

Dinner- Curried Pork Chops

Day 11

Breakfast- Sweet Potato Muffins

Lunch- Cajun Fish Fillets

Dinner- Salsa Pork Chops

Day 12

Breakfast- Broccoli Egg Breakfast Bake

Lunch- Lemon Herb Fish Fillets

Dinner- Lemon Garlic Chicken

Day 13

Breakfast- Vegetable Frittata

Lunch- Tomato Squash Zucchini Bake

Dinner- Parmesan Chicken Breasts

Day 14

Breakfast- Baked Breakfast Casserole

Lunch- Baked Fish Fillets with Pepper

Dinner- Rosemary Chicken & Potatoes

Day 15

Breakfast- Berry Baked Oatmeal

Lunch- Perfect Cheese Broccoli Bake

Dinner- Creamy Chicken

Day 16

Breakfast- Greek Egg Muffins

Lunch- Baked Balsamic Chicken

Dinner- Slow Cook Flank Steak

Day 17

Breakfast- Spinach Pepper Egg Muffins

Lunch- Tasty Smothered Chicken

Dinner- Steak & Mushrooms

Day 18

Breakfast- Healthy Spinach Frittata

Lunch- Parmesan Chicken Breasts

Dinner- Air Fryer Steak

Day 19

Breakfast- Quinoa Veggie Egg Muffins

Lunch- Rosemary Chicken & Potatoes

Dinner- Tasty Beef Fajitas

Day 20

Breakfast- Tomato Spinach Egg Muffins

Lunch- Stuffed Peppers

Dinner- Juicy Pork Chops

Day 21

Breakfast- Healthy Artichoke Frittata

Lunch- Scallop Gratin

Dinner- Honey Garlic Pork Chops

Day 22

Breakfast- Healthy Breakfast Muffins

Lunch- Dijon Salmon

Dinner- Tender Pork Loin

Day 23

Breakfast- Pumpkin Steel Cut Oats

Lunch- Flavorful Potato Casserole

Dinner- Mustard Honey Pork Chops

Day 24

Breakfast- Healthy Almond Oatmeal

Lunch- Cajun Salmon

Dinner- Herb Pork Chops

Day 25

Breakfast- Blueberry Oats

Lunch- Baked Lemon Pepper Basa

Dinner- Curried Pork Chops

Day 26

Breakfast- Sweet Potato Muffins

Lunch- Cajun Fish Fillets

Dinner- Salsa Pork Chops

Day 27

Breakfast- Broccoli Egg Breakfast Bake

Lunch- Lemon Herb Fish Fillets

Dinner- Lemon Garlic Chicken

Day 28

Breakfast- Vegetable Frittata

Lunch- Tomato Squash Zucchini Bake

Dinner- Parmesan Chicken Breasts

Day 29

Breakfast- Baked Breakfast Casserole

Lunch- Baked Fish Fillets with Pepper

Dinner- Rosemary Chicken & Potatoes

Day 30

Breakfast- Berry Baked Oatmeal

Lunch- Perfect Cheese Broccoli Bake

Dinner- Creamy Chicken

Conclusion

Air fryer ovens have been a popular kitchen gadget in the last few years because of their compact size, versatility, and capability to cook a different range of recipes into a single cooking appliance. The Emeril Lagasse Power Air Fryer 360 is one of the advanced and multipurpose cooking appliances available in the market. It is 9 in 1 cooking appliance that comes with 12-different preset functions like air fry, roast, rotisserie, bagel, pizza, slow cook, broil, warm, dehydrate, reheat, bake and toast.

This cookbook contains different types of recipes like breakfast, poultry, beef, pork & lamb, fish & seafood, vegetables & side dishes, snacks & appetizers, dehydrate, and desserts. The recipes written in this cookbook are unique and written in an easily understandable form. All the recipes are written with their preparation and cooking time with step by step cooking instructions. Each and every recipe is written in this book is ends with their nutritional value information.

9 781954 091566